ELEMENTS
OF
THE
UTOPIAN

ELEMENTS OF THE UTOPIAN

Greg S. Johnson

The Davies Group, Publishers
Aurora, Colorado

Library of Congress Cataloging-in-Publication Data

   Johnson, Greg, 1964-
    Elements of the utopian / Greg Johnson.
      p. cm.
    Includes bibliographical references.
    ISBN 978-1-934542-24-8 (alk. paper)
    1. Utopias--Philosophy. I. Title.
    HX806.J63 2010
    335'.02--dc22
                    2010041719

Printed in the United States of America
Published 2010. The Davies Group Publishers, Aurora, CO

1234567890

CONTENTS

Preface   ix

Acknowledgments   xvii

Chapter 1 The Specter of the Utopian   1

Chapter 2 The Utopian Interruption   23

Chapter 3 Forever Apart: The Bodily Element
          of the Utopian   51

Chapter 4 Forever Together: Reversibility
          and the Politics of Utopian Possibility 81

Chapter 5 Witnessing to the Utopian   113

Chapter 6 The Utopian Function of Forgiveness 145

Notes   169

Bibliography   177

Index   187

In memory of
Stearl Dotson Johnson
February 1, 1936-January 19, 2003

Ἀστὴρ πρὶν μὲν ἔλαμπες ἐνὶ ζωοῖσιν Ἐῷος,
νῦν δὲ θανὼν λάμπεις Ἕσπερος ἐν φθιμένοις.

Once among the living you shone like the morning star.
Now gone, your evening star shines among the dead.

— Plato, *Anthologia Palatina* vii 670

Preface

I remember when the utopian became existentially important to me. It was 1992. I was beginning my Masters of Theology at the Southern Baptist Theological Seminary in Louisville, Kentucky. In those days, the religious fundamentalists were gradually overtaking SBTS along with the Southern Baptist Convention as a whole. Though I could mention several issues that fashioned this early understanding of the existential importance of the utopian, I would have to point to one experience that would come to matter most in my understanding of the importance of the utopian as interruption. The issue that shaped me revolved around women classmates who after time and time again were told that they could not according to the Bible be ministers (which usually meant pastors), or were informed by more than one willing white, southern, male that they (the women) had mis-heard the call of God. Despite this these women responded knowing full well that this would mean going to what can only be described overall as a patriarchal and misogynistic environment. These women remained faithful to their calling because, it now seems clearer to me, they wanted things to be better for them and for those women who might come after them. They remained faithful to the event of their calling, among other things, by standing in the face of structural domination and degradation and, in ways they could only do, disrupted this logic that sought to oppress them. These women were, simply, utopian. To be certain, none of this came easy for them. They were berated, criticized, laughed at and many left. We did not blame them for doing so. Many, however, stayed and found ways to keep this utopian spirit alive during what were dark years for friends and certain teachers. I have come to realize that these women stand alongside the examples I will appeal to in the following chapters that instantiate my non-conventional view of the utopian. What this experience taught me is that the utopian potential can be hidden in many ways, but this potential can be unearthed and transform not only the people who experience the encounter, but also the very structures that seek to keep the utopian impulse hidden. It is against this existential backdrop that I began to think more conceptually about what a non-conventional view of the utopian might consist.

During the time of the experience mentioned above, I read Seyla Benhabib's book, *Situating the Self,* a book that would torment me with the claim that there is a practical and moral imperative to retaining the utopian. I read the book with a growing interest in critical theory, especially how this tradition could be placed into dialogue with hermeneutical philosophy in general and the thought of Paul Ricoeur in particular. If Benhabib's book would open for me the question about reconfiguring the utopian, it was Ricoeur's *Lectures on Ideology and Utopia* that would convince me that this could be done within a framework of hermeneutical phenomenology. I did not know it yet, and it would be several years before I found my way to Maurice Merleau-Ponty, but I knew at least intuitively that such a project was possible. In light of all of this, three things became apparent to me.

First, the utopian enjoyed a long history not only in political efforts, but played an equally important role in the history of philosophy. This was encouraging. I began to imagine my project contributing, albeit modestly, to the ongoing task of philosophy as a way of life. Second, as I became more familiar with both hermeneutics and phenomenology it was clear that those who aligned themselves with these traditions had virtually nothing to say about the utopian in a sustained manner, and even less to offer as a resource for beginning to understand it differently. Ironically, I decided that this was, in many respects even the case for Ricoeur. As I took up his *Lectures* more carefully, it became apparent that Ricoeur did not offer a prolonged notion of the utopian from a framework of phenomenology and hermeneutics; rather, his book engaged the utopian vis-à-vis critical social theory. This second awareness was made more pronounced when, much later on I ran across a statement by Simon Critchley who claimed that one defining trait of Continental philosophy was that it is utopian. He did not specify critical theory, but instead made this universal claim about Continental philosophy in general, which, it seemed to me had to include hermeneutics and phenomenology. This statement in particular, coupled with what I had already found in Benhabib and Ricoeur, became the inspiration for taking up the current project in a more sustained manner. In the end, while I was disappointed to find no extended treatment by those in phenomenology and hermeneutics on the nature of the utopian, I was encouraged that the utopian was thought to be of significance to Continental philosophy.

Finally, and in light of my encouragement from reading Critchley's claim, as I began to toil over how to think about and develop a conceptual notion of the utopian that could be viewed as concomitant with hermeneutical phenomenology, it was discouraging to realize that the utopian had fallen on hard times. This period, some might argue, was the highest interest in postmodern thinking that preferred the local to the general, the particular to the universal, difference to sameness and so on. It was the time of Lyotard's "incredulity toward metanarratives," of which the utopian could only be viewed as one more version. To be sure, these projects have not left us and in some respects changed the terrain upon which we think and act philosophically. The awareness of certain postmodern issues meant that my project should now not only resonate with hermeneutical phenomenology, but also take seriously the theme of situatedness in its manifestations (bodily, social, etc), yet retain the central idea that the utopian can still guide our emancipatory thinking. I surmised that even if I were able to develop such a view conceptually it would need to be a view that more concretely can be seen to be relevant to political and ethical life. This pushed me to consider moments that would give flesh to the bones of my conceptual structure. In the end, this final awareness reinforced that what I would be doing was offering a non-conventional understanding of the utopian that perhaps would look odd appealing primarily to hermeneutical phenomenology, but an understanding that nevertheless could provide a response to the deadlock created from the encounter of conventional notions of the utopian with postmodern politics of difference, a deadlock whose coordinates I refused to accept in thinking through this project. It is here that I would like to offer two caveats.

First, in what follows, I will rarely speak of Utopia and in most cases when I do, it will be in reference to someone else's use of it. To put it strongly, I am not interested in Utopia. I tend to agree with those who point out that in many important ways the belief in Utopia is responsible for some of the worst atrocities in human history. I hope it becomes clearer why I reject this idea, but here I want to say that even though I have little to no interest in Utopia (to moderate my claim) I do want to retain the kernel of truth in Utopia which I will simply refer to throughout as *the utopian*. So, perhaps it is more accurate to say I have little interest in Utopia. It would be wrong to claim that the utopian is unrelated to Utopia. What I focus on in the pages that follow, however, is what makes a belief in Utopia possible, or better what is presupposed in every Utopia. This is the utopian moment or encounter. In this regard, though they are related the utopian is not dependent on Utopia as the latter is to the former. One can be a utopian without believing in Utopia, whereas one cannot believe in Utopia without being utopian. The chapters that follow seek to develop the utopian by discussing what I claim are central elements that offer a different understanding of the utopian.

My aim is to sever the utopian from Utopia as a way of thinking differently about the very nature of the utopian itself. One can, as I will suggest, point to places where the utopian is alive without making either the theoretical or practical move to argue for Utopia in light of the utopian encounter. This, I claim, is why a focus on the elements of the utopian is significant. It retains the utopian impulse (the emancipatory nature of such thinking), and simultaneously takes seriously the situated character of all encounters to the utopian. This is not, let me emphasize, to turn universal emancipatory thinking into yet another form of localized action. It is, to the contrary, to say strongly that what makes such thinking utopian is precisely its universal message that is derived from the spaces or positions of those most secluded from ethical and political life. I suspect my universalist tendency here owes as much to Hegel's notion of "concrete universality," as it does to an early exposure to the universal message of good news in Christianity.

I am sure others will disagree with my approach that Utopia is of little to no use. I say little, again, to avoid the extreme position that Utopia and the kinds of projects that takes it up, is *a priori* incapable of being helpful. With this said, it seems even clearer to me to say that if Utopia is to be relevant in an age more and more weary of such thinking, it will have to look dramatically different than its typical use. Such a view will have to think outside of the coordinates that dictate discourse about the utopian and Utopia. This is one goal of my project.

A second caveat is related. This is a criticism about my approach that has haunted me since I first heard it, and it came in the form of a passing remark. One colleague said to me that my view was one that attempted to cheat. To this day I am not sure what he meant by this, but I think I have an idea. My hunch is that by cheating this criticism was meant to point out that what I am doing cannot in fairness be called "utopian." If this is the case, then I suppose I should agree with my colleague only insofar as we get clear first and foremost as to how we understand the utopian. My speculation would be that if one has a conventional notion of the utopian that I describe in the following pages, then my understanding, and the argument that I develop in its service, looks nothing like the utopian. This is intentional. Moreover, my claim is that the way we think about Utopia and the utopian conventionally has landed us in a deadlock about the possibilities of the utopian being relevant any longer. If we are in a deadlock, then what is needed is, again, a way of thinking that is outside of (or as much as this can be done) the coordinates that (pre)determine what we mean by the utopian, coordinates that I suggest lie behind the claim my view "cheats." If cheating means to engage resources that do not immediately come to mind in thinking about the utopian, then I plead guilty as charged. My intent is to try and move beyond this impasse in a way that does not simply repeat the coordinates that in important ways already doom any talk of the utopian. So, I would plead for patience from the reader and agree with Montaigne when he writes the following.

> I do not doubt that I often happen to talk of things which are treated better in the writings of master-craftsmen, and with more authenticity. . . . These are my own thoughts, by which I am striving to make known not matter but me. Perhaps I shall master that matter one day; or perhaps I did do so once when Fortune managed to bring me to places where light is thrown on it.... I want people to see my natural ordinary stride, however much it wanders off the path (Montaigne, 1987: 457; 459).

In the end, it is my hope that others will disagree with me and open the possibility for a more robust and relevant understanding of the utopian to emerge.

Several people deserve thanks for timely encouragement and support. I would like to begin by thanking Robert Shurden of Carson-Newman College in Jefferson City, Tennessee. Dr. Shurden formed my initial thoughts about what it means to be a college professor. He embodies all that is good about this profession, and whenever I feel as though I have accomplished something with students I remember him most of all. I owe as much to Dan Stiver of Hardin-Simmons University who was the first person to draw me to philosophy through hermeneutics. Danny was there when I struggled to make sense of philosophy in general, and Paul Ricoeur in particular. To him I am especially thankful for his continuous encouragement and his always-gentle but nonetheless critical questioning that set me on the path that introduced me to figures that appear in one way or another throughout this book. Danny, finally, was the one that suggested I leave Southern Seminary and pursue the Ph.D. elsewhere. This was, academically speaking, the best decision I made because it allowed me the opportunity to study philosophy in a more traditional environment, and more importantly to be introduced to Cheyney Ryan. When I think of the impact Cheyney has had on my thinking, it is immense. In addition to being one of the kindest people I have known, virtually every time I sit down to work out ideas, or each time I find myself asking, "What is my argument?" it is his voice that I hear, and his questions that I imagine as I attempt to produce something that I hope he could embrace. What little I have come to understand about political philosophy and its task I owe to Cheyney.

Two people factored heavily in keeping me going on this project and helped me to believe that there might be something to it. First, toward the beginning Simon Critchley responded to a paper I sent him that is now Chapter Three. I sent it to him with a note indicating how important his claim about the utopian and Continental philosophy was for my project. He wrote back a very supportive letter that, at the time, gave me confidence I needed. Toward the end of the project, I gave a version of some of the argument that follows at the Society for Phenomenology and Existential Philosophy, and Gianni Vattimo was in attendance. After this presentation, Vattimo and I talked and he showed enthusiasm for what I was doing, offered his support and wanted to read more. I am deeply grateful to both of them for simple words of encouragement. In addition, Vattimo's chief editor and collaborator, Santiago Zabala, was the one who recommended me to The Davies Group. Keith Davies has been remarkable not only for his willingness to take a risk on this project, but also for his vision of what publishing might entail. I cannot indicate enough my thanks for his patience and support.

I owe thanks to my university, which provided me with sabbatical and financial support that enabled me to work on this project. As well, my colleagues in the philosophy department here at Pacific Lutheran University deserve mentioning because they help to create an environment where I am able to flourish in ways that I believe are good. I want to give a special thanks to Kaisa Edy. Kaisa read everything more than once, offered commentary that made me rethink things, and caught many errors that would have made me look foolish. In addition, she has helped with the indexing. I could not have finished this in a timely manner without her assistance.

I owe my family a debt that cannot be calculated. My older brother, Jeffery, surprised me with a visit during the on-again, off-again nature of writing a book. He showed me that not all interruptions are bad. My younger sister, Beverly, is someone who probably knows me as well as anyone, and has always shown appreciation for what I do, why

I do it and why it has taken me away from my family. From her I am learning more about determination, perseverance and equanimity in the face of trying times. My Momma, Esta Leel Reed Johnson, is a daily inspiration. She does not know it, but when I first read Merleau-Ponty and others on the primacy of "embodied knowledge," my instinct was not to go to the history of philosophy. It was, instead, to recollect how she would cook without recipes, figure things out without predetermined guidelines, and utilize all of the "embodied" things it took for her to be a professional cook that she was. She has also demonstrated to me like no other than while it is easy to give up in the face of adversity and suffering, going on and through such events makes a difference in the task of becoming a self. To my Daddy, Stearl, I dedicate this book. Like my Mother, I learned from him that what I would come to define as the task of living philosophically was already an idea he exhibited in terms of living ones life in the service of holding on to the threads of existence, and at other times being joyful that you made it through to do well. Although he never quite understood what being a teacher of philosophy involved, the question he asked me a lot, "Now, *what* is it you do?" hovers over this book and my work. To Nancy I owe gratitude for being there in ways that always make a difference. And, to Benjamin, now 12, who upon being asked by his then third grade teacher (who knew I taught Philosophy) if his dad would like to be a participant in their version of *Are You Smarter than a Third-Grader?* replied: "My dad doesn't know a lot, but he is good at philosophy." I can't think of an endorsement I would prefer more.

Acknowledgments

For permission to use previously published material, I would like to acknowledge the following publishers:

"Johnny Cash: Philosophy as a Way of Life, in *Johnny Cash and Philosophy: The Burning Ring of Truth*, edited by John Huss and David Werther, *Popular Culture and Philosophy Series* Volume 31, Chicago, Il.: Open Court Publishing, 2008; "Merleau-Ponty, Reciprocity and the Reversibility of Perspectives," in *Intertwinings: Reflections on Maurice Merleau-Ponty*, edited by Gail Weiss, State University of New York Press 2008; "On the Place of Reversibility in Deliberative Democracy," *Social Philosophy Today*, Volume 19, 2004; "Merleau-Pontian Phenomenology as Non-Conventionally Utopian," *Human Studies*,Vol. 26 Issue 3, 2003; "The Economies of Grace as Gift and Moral Accounting: Insights from Cognitive Linguistics," in *The Bible through Metaphor and Translation: A Cognitive Semantic Perspective*. Eds. Kurt Feyaerts and Dirk Geeraerts. (Peter Lang Press, 2003). "The Situated Self and Utopian Thinking," *Hypatia: A Journal of Feminist Philosophy*, Vol. 17, No. 3 Summer, 2002.

Chapter One

The Specter of the Utopian

Our present utopian needs are probably best met by philosophical writing which is straight-forwardly unfictional, but imaginative nevertheless. On the other hand, our needs will not be met by blueprints, by schemes too specific in detail.... Rather, we need bold utopian thought that is general and radical, that builds on novel capacities and takes the measure of novel problems, but goes beyond them in its exploration of the human condition and the requirements for at least approximating utopia.

—George Kateb (1971: 23-24)

The necessary utopian moment in feminism lies precisely in our opening up the possible through metaphoric transformation. . . . Here, I am using utopia in a more traditional way, but not in the sense of the establishment of a blueprint of an ideal society. Utopian thinking demands the continual exploration and re-exploration of the possible and yet also unrepresentable. . . . Without utopian thinking . . . feminism is inevitably ensnared in the system of gender identity that devalues the feminine.

—Drucilla Cornell (1991: 169)

These are powerful statements on behalf of utopian thinking. If, however, one looks around the world and sees the pervasive existence of violence, war and atrocities inflicted in the name of one country toward another, reconsidering the utopian probably seems an exercise in futility. To begin I want to pose the question "Why the utopian?" Once I offer a response to this question, I will then turn to an overview of my argument and indicate how I propose to reconsider the utopian.

First, it seems simple enough to claim that we need the utopian because as the arm of critique it empowers us to transcend situations that threaten to destroy us. It gives us the impetus to change them and keeps us moving toward ever-new alternatives for being together. In this regard, we might say that the utopian, to borrow a line from Martin Luther King Jr.'s words, is a "movement based on hope" (King, 1991a: 52). King, like those quoted above, knew we could not do without the utopian. As he illustrated, utopian thinking might arise from a *specific* need but it ultimately affects *all* people, which is why the utopian, at its best, is universalistic in scope. Such thinking infused King's dream, his vision of society. We know these words:

> A dream of equality, of opportunity, of privilege and property widely distributed; a dream of a land where men no longer argue that the color of a man's skin determines the content of his character; the dream of a land where every man will respect the dignity and worth of human personality—this is the dream (King, 1991b: 105).

He recognized the importance of the utopian as the dream able to move multitudes to go beyond the degrading and dehumanizing system of racism. It was a dream, in Kateb's words, which was "general and radical and built on novel capacities." More importantly, it was a dream, though not realized, that inspired King and others to risk their very lives.

Second, the utopian at its best is about ethical and political transformation, not about naïve escapism, though it could become such. Once more, I would suggest that King understood this:

> There is a danger, therefore, that after hearing of all of this [talk about the coming of a new age] that you will go away with the impression that we can go home, sit down, and do nothing, waiting for the coming of the inevitable. You will somehow feel that this new age will roll in on the wheels of inevitability, so there is nothing to do but wait on it. If you get that impression you are the victims of an illusion wrapped in superficiality. We must speed up the coming of the inevitable (King, 1991c: 141).

THE SPECTER OF THE UTOPIAN

The utopian requires hard work, determination and the capacity to persevere. Even though King embraced utopian thinking he was well aware of the potential traps it possessed. Just as such thought can move people to risk their lives it can as easily depoliticize and trivialize their action. Just as it can open us to new potentialities it can also close in on itself and cause movement to become static and paralyzing. It seems, however, that in our ever-present preoccupation with "post-metaphysical" thinking we have thrown out the baby of utopian politics with the bath water of naïve escapism. In effect, to label someone "utopian" is to suggest that they are, at best, naïve and disconnected or, at worst, just plain mad.

"Utopian" has come to mean those who, to use King's words, suffer from "an illusion wrapped in superficiality." More specifically, the utopian is now most often associated with the kind of thinking that "presupposes a form of philosophical idealism that inevitably results in a mystification that ignores difference, flux, dissemination and heterogeneity" (West, 1993: 166). If this is all that the utopian means, then the dismissal of the utopian is undoubtedly correct. Such a view, however, is not only a narrow understanding, but is a far cry from the utopian politics of King and those I quoted at the beginning of the chapter.

One would think that political philosophers in particular could see this. But we are no different. We have, for the most part, forgotten that the utopian as a political mode of action keeps open the space of critique. Thus, in our refusal to retain the utopian impulse we have acquiesced to those who narrowly define the utopian as that which solely means indifference to difference. I say "for the most part" because some thinkers, in the spirit of Kateb, King and others, have called for a renegotiation of the utopian, freeing it from fixed, static visions that seek unity at the expense of difference. In particular, I am referring to the work of Drucilla Cornell and Seyla Benhabib, both of whom speak of the need to rethink the utopian as "a practical and moral imperative" (Benhabib, 1992: 229), or that which is a "turn toward the future" that "has already begun" (Cornell, 1992: 188; 129). The difference between these thinkers and those who want to homogenize what it means to be utopian is that they acknowledge the critical and constructive dimension of utopian thought while also recognizing its pathological tendencies. That is to say, they accept the dual nature of utopian thinking. On the one hand, it can become "an illusion wrapped in superficiality." On the other hand, as Benhabib and Cornell illustrate, the politics of the utopian can also be viewed as "an 'opening' to the beyond as a threshold we are invited to cross" (Cornell, 1992: 110). In short, theirs is a call to retrieve the ethical impulse of the utopian that so infused King and other transformative political movements. Viewed in the narrower light it is understandable why we might refuse to renegotiate the utopian. It is easier to define it narrowly and dismiss it than to wrestle with and retrieve it. If this is the case, then it is no wonder that the question "Why the utopian?" would be asked. There are, as one guess, a variety of strategies to retrieve the utopian for which Benhabib, Cornell, and Kateb call.

A first strategy, as I indicate above, is to dismiss it as mere naïve escapism. Such thinking, so the argument goes, lacks any relevance because it is otherworldly and disconnected from life's struggles. Second, and related, we could bypass the utopian because, as irrelevant, it is in the end nonsense and counterproductive. The irrelevancy has to do with viewing the utopian as opposed to philosophy in a more applied manner. To be utopian is to be in the "no-place" that is disconnected from the realities that define our lives. I will, in chapters that follow, argue against this view. Finally, we can think through what it might mean to be utopian in our contemporary setting. By thinking through I mean that we begin to think the unthought of the utopian moment, which helps to break the coordinates that have caused the utopian to become deadlocked and irrelevant. This means, I suggest, exploring resources that may not initially look utopian at all. Additionally, the task is to retrieve the utopian in a way that does not fetishize it, but instead reconfigures it so that the "not-yet" realized horizon of potentialities binds us together and gives us an impetus for action in a way that is not solely pathological. My claim is that explored through the traditions of phenomenology and hermeneutics this retrieval will refuse a simple reiteration of the past. The analysis of the utopian from within these orientations can expose the new and often hidden possibilities latent in the label "utopian" that enables us to repeat the utopian in our own context. (See Heidegger, 1959: 39; 191).[1]

Let me return to the pressing question "Why the utopian?" There are at least two reasons that begin to answer this question. First, the utopian provides the critical impetus that empowers our transformative ethics and politics. As the single most important liberatory effort of the twentieth century, the civil rights movement was infused with a sense of the utopian, a sense that disrupted traditional and societal understandings of equality, freedom and respect. Second, without utopian thinking the possibility of such transformative politics wanes because the claims of the discourse of situatedness, while making us aware of our own particularities, can easily lead to a parochialism that is politically impotent. To illustrate further these two reasons let us consider the following example where the utopian impulse is often considered a central element of liberatory praxis: the women's movement in general and feminist theory in particular.

Although not all feminist thinkers see value in the utopian, the fact that many feminist theorists call for a retrieval of the utopian impulse should raise our awareness of the need for such thought.[2] Let me say why this is the case by considering the following examples. First, Toril Moi speaks to the more general interest in the utopian while Benhabib, my second example, addresses the particularities of such thinking.

Moi writes that "to deprive feminism of its utopias is to depoliticize it at a stroke: without a political vision to sustain it, feminist theory will hit a dead end. The result will be a loss of purpose, a perfect sense of futility, and the transformation of feminism into a self-perpetuating academic institution like any other" (Moi, 1993: 352). Like utopian thinkers in the past who recognized its strengths for political thought, feminist theorists "need the wider scope afforded by utopianism to express their conception of society fully" (Goodwin, 1991: 537). Second, Benhabib, as I have already said, thinks that utopian thinking is a practical-moral imperative. She further claims that there is no need to retreat unnecessarily from the ideal of the utopian as many suggest. She maintains that such a reluctance to rethink the role of the utopian on the part of feminist undermines their own commitments to important issues such as woman's agency, selfhood, and most importantly "women's own history in the name of an emancipated future." "We, as women," she concludes, "have much to lose by giving up the utopian hope in the wholly other" (Benhabib, 1992: 229-230). This embrace of the utopian on the part of many feminist political philosophers is perhaps shocking especially if we associate the utopian impulse with a fixed, static understanding. Why, then, am I focusing here on *feminist* political philosophers?

Feminist theorists have every reason to be suspect of the utopian, especially the traditional forms that allegedly eradicate difference. It may seem strange to us that if utopian thinking were the great example of totalizing and homogenizing thinking, then feminist theorist's adoption of such thinking would undermine their own efforts at situated critique. Said more strongly, to embrace the utopian understood in this manner would be to incorporate a form of thought opposed to much, if not all, of feminist theory, an orientation that in all of its plurality is generally concerned with theorizing difference as constitutive of our identity. For instance, analysis influenced by feminist theory can take the specific form of exploring gender differences where the categories of male/man and female/woman are problematized. Or, such analysis can take as its emphasis difference as a more general category where gender difference is of but one important aspect. The point at which both emphases converge is the importance of acknowledging difference(s) as the starting point for any political interaction instead of the erasure of difference(s) for some disembodied common human experience. Finally, to embrace the utopian in its conventional understanding would be to disregard present situations. If there is one thing feminist theorists have consistently emphasized it is the necessity of working *here and now* instead of being preoccupied with something detached from our lived existence. Thus, the utopian as that which implies the transcending of differences and situations in the name of an overarching future unity could potentially undermine this emphasis that, consequently, would be anathema to feminist concerns for the present. Why, then, are feminist theorists like Benhabib and Cornell calling us to reconsider the utopian impulse?

First, they see in utopian thought a political value that retains a vision for the liberatory efforts of women. As Moi suggests, without this kind of distinct political vision the emancipatory work of feminism can easily become itself irrelevant and unaware of situatedness *as* an event of transformative politics. Second, and most important for my purposes, while they value the utopian impulse they nevertheless imply a different understanding of utopian thought, one that retains the traditional impetus of the utopian while suggesting the possibility of an alternative understanding. I will, therefore, reject what I will call throughout the book a *conventional* understanding of the utopian and instead offer in its place an alternative account that is inspired by Benhabib and others.

To be sure, I have intentionally remained general in designating this naïve escapist view as traditional or conventional. What I want to do in the following section is, first, offer a brief account of salient features of the traditional view along with why I reject it and, second, offer an overview of the view I will argue for more specifically in the remaining chapters.

I want to begin with a general description of the conventional understanding of the utopian, and indicate why I will reject this view. First, there is a colloquial understanding of utopian thought that is captured in the *Oxford English Dictionary* when it states that such thinking revolves around a "place, state, or condition ideally perfect in respect of politics, laws, customs and conditions. . . . [Utopia is] an impossibly ideal scheme, especially for social improvement." If there is one primary characteristic of the utopian, as this definition attests, it is that such thought has as its goal a state of perfection (Utopia). More specifically, it is that which seeks to encompass and bring everything under the same unifying principle/vision. Thus, the colloquial understanding is perhaps best expressed by the phrase "pie-in-the-sky," which usually signifies a perfect state other than the imperfect state in which we now live.

The technical definition parallels the colloquial one offered above and is best described by Barbara Goodwin who writes that utopianism is "a unique method of reflecting on politics and society, which seeks the perfect, best, or happiest form of society, untrammeled by commitments to existing institutions" (Goodwin, 1991: 533). There are, then, at least two ways to summarize the conventional view of the utopian. On the one hand, to be utopian is to think out of the situation one finds oneself in, and think instead into a perfected state that is "untrammeled" by that situation. On the other hand, to be utopian is to employ the imaginative in the service of abstraction that ideally orients our thinking about what constitutes the well-ordered society, the individual, and so forth. From these general features, we can see more clearly how traditional utopian thought develops around three foci: form, content, and function. I will reject the first two elements, and adopt, albeit in an expanded way in the next chapter, the third characteristic.[3]

The form of utopian thinking has historically been construed within the bounds of literary genre. The form is said to be primarily imaginary or fictional. Here, for example, More's *Utopia* and Campanella's *The City of the Sun* are exemplary. This is not to deny that fictional works that illustrate this category are devoid of any political import. What is highlighted, rather, is the picture-making quality of the utopian. To reduce the utopian to this understanding, however, is problematic because,

> [De]pictions of the good society do not necessarily take the form of literary fictions—and indeed this form is only available under certain very specific historical conditions; is it then to be assumed that when these conditions do not exist there are no utopias?"(Levitas, 1990: 5).

The utopian, then, is one who participates in fiction or fantasy that constructs picture images of alternative worlds.[4] Moreover, as an instance of our imaginative capacities, especially our productive imaginative capacities, utopian thought is believed to have instructive value insofar as such thinking is to make us better, more just, more fair, etc. Whether one regards utopian thought as merely didactic or more than this, the significant point of this discussion is that to the degree that they are by definition fictions, utopian thinking on this account differs from historical writing because the former deals with possible worlds instead of actual ones (cf. Kumar, 1991). The point here is not so much the role of the imagination in the utopian (something I wish to retain), but how this kind of work historically functions as a "blueprint" model, which possesses at least three characteristics.

First, the blueprint model *produces a vision* of how society should be best ordered so that this ordering can, once established, insure that citizens will act in ways in accordance to the model itself. Such a view runs from typical understandings of Plato's *Republic* to contemporary Human Rights discourse. For instance, building on the work of John Rawls (whose *Theory of Justice* is paradigmatic in this case), Thomas Pogge's essay "How Should Human Rights Be Conceived," starts with the notion that before we can talk about rights themselves, or how to secure these rights, we *first* must organize society in such a way that then makes defining and securing rights possible (See Pogge, 2001:187-210). Second, this model *offers a method* for insuring that all members can participate (or at least potentially do so) in the blueprint and in doing so bring about the actualization of the possibility inherent in the model itself. A good example here is the way one might read Rousseau's *The Social Contract* together with his *Emile*. The two are disparate treatises on the role of the community/general will and the civic man. Rousseau's *Emile* is a book that demonstrates how individuals will participate in the *Social Contract* such that the general will can then produce civilized individuals. Whereas the *Contract* is the model, the *Emile* is the method by which the individual participates in and creates the ideal indicated in the *Contract*. Finally, inherent in the blueprint model is a *way to resolve conflict*. It is not an understatement to say that conventional utopian thought overwhelmingly assumes that if the model is accepted, and the individuals embrace the method, then this will lead to a state of peaceful co-existence where there is at best the absence of conflict, and, at worst conflict that can be resolved by an appeal to the model/method themselves. I will reject this blueprint model, along with its form and content fixation, for the following reasons.

First, on this model, the utopian is or becomes a type of purified thought devoid of the structures that mark our need to take up the questions that motivate the utopian in the first place. The move to the abstract discussed above creates an understanding of the project of the utopian that while beginning with lived experience, soon becomes *dis*-embedded from the situations that give rise to the need for the utopian in the first place. I will, in later chapters, argue that the universal dimension of the utopian inherent in the blueprint model is worth retaining, a notion of the universal that is different from the abstraction that causes the utopian to become irrelevant. Here is why this is significant.

It could easily be argued that most if not all utopian thinkers initially present themselves as revolutionaries whose visions can transform society. However, what soon becomes the case, either with the original utopian thinker or his or her followers, is that the utopian quest ends up a quest for a fixed point on the horizon at which we aim. As Goodwin intimates above, this fixed point is thought to be a point unencumbered by the particularities of one's existence. Thus, what characterizes this utopian horizon is uniformity where all differences are erased for sameness. The difference between the former revolutionary thinkers and the latter whose utopian politics become fixed and static is the moment of pathology where utopian thought ceases to be utopian and becomes ideology. To put it in terms I will return to in the next chapter, it is the movement where thought no longer interrupts but instead reaffirms what is already taken for granted. While all utopian thinkers may begin as thinkers who are critical of the powers that be, many utopian projects and the accompanying ideas become fixed, and consequently immaterial to the lives of those solicited by the utopian. In this precise way, such projects become naïve escape mechanisms that function as a "mystificatory ideology as soon as it justifies the oppression of today in the name of liberation tomorrow" (Kearney, 1984: 28). It is no surprise then that the utopian is rejected because "from this politics of perfection springs the politics of uniformity; a scheme which does not recognize circumstance can have no place for variety" (Oakeshott, 1977: 5-6). Let's come back to Rousseau.

Keeping in mind what I have already said about him, Rousseau's normative utopian project in the text *On the Government of Poland* begins with one's existence in the world and relies on both experience and interaction. Soon, however, *The Social Contract* replaces the individual will with the will of the whole. This displacement is accomplished by education, illustrated by the *Emile*, where human nature becomes re-made. What is presented in all of this is a rationally worked out plan to attain human freedom in the form of "civil man." But in this process the individual's own particularity is sacrificed for the will of the whole. And even though Rousseau begins with our existence, he still engages in a positing of the autonomous male ego as that which defines all other subjectivities, hence ignoring certain particularities (especially those of women).

To be fair, Rousseau exemplifies the spectrum of utopian thinking insofar as we can affirm his project of the critique of existing society yet reject his turn to the *Social Contract*, which presents a better society that *can be perfected* in and through the actualization of the contract. If this were the only picture of utopian thinking we had it would make perfect sense to question its relevance for contemporary use, as Ralf Dahrendorf does in the following passage.

> Utopia is in the nature of the idea of a total society. It may exist 'nowhere,' but it is held up as a counterproject to the realities of the world in which we are living. Utopia is a complete alternative, and therefore of necessity a complete society.... Whoever sets out to implement Utopian plans will in the first instance have to wipe clean the canvas on which the real world is painted. This is a brutal process of destruction. Second, a new world will have to be constructed which is bound to lead to errors and failures, and will in any case require awkward transitional periods like 'dictatorship of the proletariat.' The probability must be high that in the end we will be stuck with the transition; dictators

are not in the habit of giving up their power (Dahrendorf, 1990: 61-62).

Dahrendorf echoes my point above that a conventional view of the utopian is motivated by perfection and uniformity. In addition to what I say, however, he highlights what he thinks is a destructive dimension to traditional utopian thinking that, as I will argue in the next chapter, can be seen as part of its central function. This emphasis on the destructive capacity of utopian thought is also echoed by Leonidis Donskis who writes that "The objective of utopian thinking, then, is to be deconstructive as opposed to constructive" (Donskis, 1996: 203). Donskis (and to a lesser degree Dahrendorf) overstates the case here because the utopian, while it is certainly deconstructive in that it problematizes our conventional understandings of reality, is also, as I will demonstrate in subsequent chapters, constructive because it creates a potential whereby *universal* transformation is intended. The issue, of course, is just what one means by "constructive." If this means providing an alternative blueprint, then those who reject the utopian as irrelevant are, in my estimation, correct. That one offers a blueprint, for instance, for making society and its participants more inclusive, more tolerant, and so on still (as often in the case of science fiction) illustrates the blueprint model of the utopian. This should be rejected because the blueprint model is of no use in positing an alternative to an alternative that itself is already a blueprint. If, however, construction is opening the space for alternative potentialities that themselves are realistic to the political conditions that define our lived existence, then the utopian is, as I have been suggesting and hope to show as this book proceeds, relevant to ethical and political life. The relevancy, to be sure, is not that it projects something fixed, able to methodically produce the preferred kinds of participants, and able to magically erase conflict. Nor is its relevancy the process of becoming utopian. The relevancy lies in the fact that the utopian will, as much as possible, *specify* the particular response(s) to a particular situation(s). Doing otherwise might be good for thought experiments, but they are simply useless to the realities of political life that the utopian, at its best, attempts to address.

The problem with emphasizing the form in utopian thinking is, in the end, that insofar as it is constructive it is a construction that often, especially in modern utopian projects, presupposes a fixed, rationally worked-out plan that can be implemented. If our principal understanding is one in which the utopian is concerned with positing a static horizon against which we move and have our being, then it is little wonder that such thinking is either rejected completely or deemed highly suspect. Such thought, as we have seen, would be thought that seeks totalization, the unification of differences, and complete consensus. Consequently, utopian thinking so construed is thought where closure, consummation and a need for actualization are our guides rather than interruption that unearths potential utopian alternatives to lived existence. The form of the utopian, however, is by itself unable to describe fully the traditional understanding. We also need content.

The content question is straightforward: "What *is* utopian thought?" The answer sometimes comes by distinguishing utopian thought from other types. The problem is not so much that the utopian society is distinct from other types of societies, but rather utopian society has been regarded as that which is possible, fixed, perfectible, and understood via a rationally worked-out blueprint for translating the future into the present. It is in this preoccupation with the "what" of utopian thought that reveals its detrimental aspects, namely, a superlative state that "must be considered beyond the reach of necessity of change, since there is no progressing beyond the perfect" (Goodwin, 1978: 5). When this persistence of the "what" of utopian thinking takes over, fixity and finality take precedent at the expense of what I have been calling the utopian potential. Fixity and finality in these blueprint models are designed to absorb and thereby eradicate all contentious particulars that threaten the worked out plan, rational or otherwise, that the blueprint ensures. In addition, as we will see more below, this move to fixity and absorption is precisely the moment of pathology where the original utopian impulse is translated into a blueprint for society designed to unify and, I want to suggest, cover over the very utopian impulse that generates such thinking. This movement toward stasis is why utopian thought becomes irrelevant; it no longer relates to the existence that originally gave rise to the utopian moment. How then does the content relate to the perfect state at which we aim? The content demarcates the perfection. For instance, the content can contain the blueprint that indicates both how we can attain the state of perfection, or, for example, the methods by which this perfect world can be attained. Therefore, the form of utopian thought, as a picture image, is useless without the content of such thinking (the details that bring the image(s) together). This is a view that, in the end, has as its goal either through process or destination some sense of the content of the utopian vision being actualized. I will, likewise, reject this view for the following reasons.

The utopian that relies on the kind of content discussed above (and the form it presupposes) is one that emphasizes a movement of such thinking, but in such a way that emphasizes how possibility is actualized. The problem is that such thinking gives way to a rigid teleology that portends to direct all possibility into realized actuality. In doing so, the utopian is one who privileges such actualizable content at the expense of the conditions in which the need for the utopian first arises. In this way, the utopian that invokes the particular kind of content/form container and views the form as that which in some way methodologically guarantees the content is a trait of the utopian that cuts across genres from the Millenarianism of the 16th Century to so-called feminist science fiction. In these cases, what is common is the belief in some world other than the one we inhabit as the proper site of the utopian. As we will see later on, the utopian is that mode of political engagement with the less than ideal (dare I even say miserable) conditions that mark the existence of those who, in an instant, become the bearers of the utopian. Such thinking, to be sure, can give way to tendencies I am describing here, but what will remain consistent in the view that I am developing is that the utopian is not other worldly in the sense that he or she is removed from the material conditions that define our lives. Rather, the utopian is one who responds to the conditions into which we are thrown and those with which we find ourselves "out-of-joint." It will be this moment of being "out-of-joint" as the moment of the utopian that will be my focus in subsequent chapters.

The point I am emphasizing here is that when the utopian focuses on a process of actualizing the possible the utopian is as apt to become pathological as those who more straightforwardly claim this kind of movement toward stasis is the goal. Why? Because the value of the utopian in this understanding "lies not in its relation to present practice but in its relation to a possible future. Its 'practical' use is to overstep the immediate reality to depict a condition whose clear desirability draws us on, like a magnet" (Kumar, 1991: 3). This statement echoes much of what I have been saying throughout this chapter. Kumar's description summarily highlights two elements of the conventional view that I have here been developing in terms of form and content. First, the utopian posits a fixed horizon, "a magnet," that draws us. Second, due to the static nature of the content presented, the utopian in this way focuses in the future present than the immediate present. Kumar adds a telling statement when he says that what unites utopians and gives utopian theory its distinctive emphasis is "the assumption that there is nothing in [human], nature or society that cannot be so ordered as to bring about a more or less permanent state of material plenty, social harmony and individual fulfillment" (Kumar, 1991: 29). To Kumar's credit he does mention qualities of the utopian that will factor prominently in my own account. It is his retention of notions such as complete harmony and design defined in terms of perfection and stasis that are those I want to reject.

Let me summarize what I have argued so far. There are at least two main reasons why utopian thinking has come under attack in recent years. First, when we hear the word "utopia" or "utopian" we almost automatically think of something that is otherworldly, escapist or that which can be perfected in actualization. Even though utopian thinkers might have begun with intentions of transforming their situations (and even this is debatable), such visions of a better world soon became pathological. The example I offered is Rousseau. Second, utopian thinking engages in universalistic thinking. Even though I will say more about this idea later on, let me here add the following.

As that which is universalistic in its thrust, utopian thinking can be thought of as exemplary of metanarrative thought (cf. Lyotard, 1984). On this understanding, then, utopian thought is viewed as incompatible with various forms of contextualism, most of which rule out any type of universalism. Such thinking is unacceptable for many because one cannot privilege situatedness or particularity and still talk of universalism. I will argue, however, that one can do this and in doing so puts the utopian on a different footing. But, before we can see this, it will be helpful to indicate the trajectory of the overall argument.

My argument, in general, proceeds along two general trajectories. First, I develop a *conceptual* understanding of the utopian that is simultaneously fully situated yet still able to guide emancipatory thinking and practice. In addition, there will be a constant reference to *concrete practices* that epitomize certain elements of my non-conventional view with the final chapter developing a concrete instance of utopian politics that embodies all of the elements for which I argue. My aim in providing this continual reference to concrete practices is to demonstrate how the utopian as I understand it is relevant to ethical and political life.

In the following chapter I develop the central element of my understanding of the utopian: the *interruptive*. As I argue, the interruptive dimension of the utopian signals the moment or the instant at which the utopian demand that things be better emerges. I will demonstrate this element by showing the two ways of understanding the moment of the utopian interruption. The *encounter* with the utopian is that which shatters our given understandings of a whole host of things personal, social, political and so on. This moment, I show, is one that is best understood as an *advent* that comes to us, yet demands of us a response. I develop this element in terms of the way we conceptualize morality, and how something like the utopian moment of grace disrupts this way of thinking and acting as the alternative of grace emerges in context with the conceptual metaphor of moral accounting. The goal here is to show that at the heart of the utopian is the interruptive moment that demands of us something in the service of the demand that things be different. In this initial encounter with the utopian, non-conventionally understood, we begin to see the revolutionary potential (again) of the utopian that has made it such an important component to the lived experience of its proponents.

My point of departure in Chapter Three is two passing remarks. The first is by Northrop Frye who claimed that in the future the utopian would be rooted in the body. The second is by Simon Critchley who makes what I contend is a startling claim that all of Continental philosophy including phenomenology and hermeneutics is utopian. Against these remarks, which function for me as a challenge, I turn to what I call the bodily element of the utopian. In particular, I take both Frye and Critchley seriously and turn to the phenomenology of Maurice Merleau-Ponty to argue for this bodily element of the utopian. My argument here is that lived bodily experience is the site, in many instances, for the interruptive in-breaking of the utopian described in chapter two.

The majority of the chapter, first, deals with establishing the claim that utopian thought—like all thought—has its roots in our lived bodily existence, a link that not only allows us to see how the utopian can be fully situated but also reveals how phenomenology and the utopian can be thought together. Second, to make my argument concrete and show how a phenomenological view provides an understanding of how the utopian is carried in and through lived bodily existence, I consider the nineteenth-century abolitionist Sojourner Truth, in particular her speech "Ain't I a Woman?" In opposition to the dehumanizing narratives within nineteenth-century America, Truth's own embodied experience accomplishes something that normative political philosophies of her time are unable to do, which is to take seriously bodily phenomena as the locus for engaging oppression and constructing alternative pictures of reality. This example, I conclude, illustrates the phenomenological insights that lived bodily existence *is* the basis for what can legitimately be called her utopian demand that things be better, an example that bears out both Frye's and Critchley's claims. In light of the element of embodiment detailed in chapter three, however, a question begins to emerge. This is: "What becomes of collective utopian efforts?"

Put in the language of chapter three the question can be formulated in this way: If the body is an important element for reconfiguring the utopian, and you have multiple bodies, then how do so many bodies work together in a collectively utopian manner? This question, left unattended, will all but leave my non-conventional understanding of the utopian on the dust heap of sophomoric relativism, and thus undermine the very aspect of the utopian I intend to retain, namely, its ability to reorient us in transformative ways we deem worthy of pursuit by others. To address this question, "What becomes of *collective* efforts?" I turn again to the work of Merleau-Ponty, this time his later work.

In Chapter Four I develop what I call the element of reversibility. This notion allows us to think simultaneously the transformative power of the utopian but not at the expense of the concerns of difference and otherness. In general, I show how we can hold these tensions together but it requires a *phenomenological understanding of the reversibility of perspectives*, which I derive from the later work of Merleau-Ponty. After I trace the emergence of the issue of reversibility in contemporary thinking, I argue that this phenomenological notion of reversibility can then be understood as an important element of the utopian. In particular, I advance the following claims.

First, reversibility evokes the idea of mutuality but not of complete and perfect mutuality. It reveals the web of co-existence we have with each other as well as the environments of which we are all a part. Second, reversibility participates in and opens the question of universality, a universality that, in the light of reversibility, resists violent forms of totalizing explanation. In this way I show that because of the moment of alterity summoned by reversibility, sharing, to the degree of absorbing unity (as a response to the fear of instability), or unanimous consensus among us before agreement is possible are problematized. The differences that bind us can as easily fracture us, but this need not preclude *a priori* the collective efforts under a new sign of the utopian. Finally, I conclude by claiming that a notion of reversibility understood in the way I develop it is preferable to notion of reciprocity, in particular as it is understood in theories of deliberative democracy. By preference here I maintain that even if one places reciprocity central to a theory about political life, reciprocity presupposes a form of reversibility that, I conclude, makes reciprocity possible. The notion of reversibility, coupled with the element of embodiment argued for in Chapter Three, allows us to understand how the utopian can simultaneously remain situated and still open the place of universality, a combination that is the utopian at its best.

Chapter Five addresses the question "How do we represent the utopian?" More specifically, the question that emerges is in the light of the disruption that occurs with the utopian, which is an advent that is still structured by lived bodily experience and reversibility, is how do we speak about this encounter, this interruption? In this chapter, my claim is that we do so in terms of being a responsible witness. A responsible witness, I argue, possesses certain characteristics vis-à-vis the utopian, and begins with providing testimony on behalf of the utopian.

First, and more generally, I rely on Paul Ricoeur's notion of a "hermeneutics of testimony" to understand the interpretive dimension of testimony. The orienting claim here will be that the utopian is a demand that is to be interpreted and yet that which interprets us. As such, it requires a witness. To speak of the utopian as that which relies on a hermeneutics of testimony, then, is to say at least that the utopian is about how we represent the truthfulness of the advent that has laid a claim on our lives. It, moreover, raises the issue of how this vision that is different is represented and in what ways we best signify what we believe to be the truthfulness of its content. This notion of interpretation, further, extends the discussion begun in Chapter Four, which is the notion of the universal. In this chapter, the universal becomes a mode by which we witness to the utopian, a witness who intends claims brought by the utopian, and claims on whose benefit we now speak. To speak universally is to recognize that the utopian carries with it a call to engage the world with its emancipatory message. To illustrate what I mean, I introduce the reader to "integrative feminisms," which is guided by utopian goals grounded in women-centered perspectives that contribute to the larger transformation of the world. As such, it brings together the notions of reversibility, universal intent and the way utopian politics arises from particular locations. It also raises the question of how we might understand engagement as a form of witnessing to the utopian.

Accordingly, Chapter Five offers two options that provide resources for considering what it means to engage the world as witnesses on behalf of the utopian. First, I again employ the work of Simon Critchley and combine it with the element of reversibility in the previous chapter. This mode of engagement, as a phenomenology of reversibility will show, takes place *in between* the space of ultimate certainty and paralysis brought on by some forms of politics of difference. I will make use of Critchley's notion of *interstitial engagement*. Second, I offer as a resource the recent work of Gianni Vattimo, who has also called for a reconsideration of the utopian as significant to emancipatory politics. Vattimo enables us to see that engagement is about learning to live in the absence of ultimate criteria that once might have functioned to do the work of engaging conflicting accounts, which a witness to the utopian will undoubtedly encounter, but that have now lost their ability to deliver on what they promise. This ability to engage others on behalf of the utopian requires certain traits that I will suggest can be of use to the one who witnesses to the utopian. In the light of all of this, I will argue that there are traits of a responsible witness to the utopian. With the above in mind, I will highlight three characteristics of the responsible witness. These are fidelity to the event, truthfulness, and consistency in action. I will argue that these characteristics flow from the notion of testimony that orients the first part of the chapter. With this chapter complete, the elements of my understanding of the utopian are in place. In the final chapter, I will argue that such thinking is far from irrelevant. To the contrary, I will contend that we can see these elements of the utopian at work by considering a recent political movement that, despite its flaws, reflects the utopian at its best.

Chapter Six considers the work of the South African Truth and Reconciliation Commission as an instance of the utopian delineated in previous chapters. Highlighting along the way the connection between the TRC and my non-conventional view enables me to show how a transformative movement such as the TRC allows for the possibility of the return of the utopian demand that things be different. I do not, it should be emphasized, accept *in toto* all of the TRC's efforts and indicate, where appropriate, why this is the case. Instead, I argue that it is the TRC's insistence that "there is no future without forgiveness" that challenges our deeply held beliefs not only about retributive justice, but the kind of theorizing that provides the conceptual support for such views (i.e., deliberative democracy). To this end, I argue for what I will call the "utopian function of forgiveness," highlighting the story of Amy Biehl who was murdered in South Africa and whose assailants were granted amnesty by the TRC with the blessing of Amy's parents. What becomes clear is that the TRC's reliance on forgiveness provides us with an example of how the utopian interrupts the need for certain models of justice that are potentially outdated, a notion of the utopian that is figured by the embodied lives of those intertwined, a view that relies specifically on the notion of reversibility, and a view that illustrates the way we engage the world and witness to the utopian demand that things be different. Such a proposal, however, is not without criticism. I conclude this chapter by taking up the criticism of the TRC by those who do not see this work as sufficiently the work of justice. In particular, I show how theorists of deliberative democracy resist the work of the TRC on these grounds. In response, I show how such a view is mistaken and as such has the effect of covering over the utopian impulse in the work of the TRC instead of cultivating or participating in it. The goal here is to show that with the TRC the utopian is not only relevant, but always a risk worth taking in thought and action born from an interruption.

Chapter Two

The Utopian Interruption

In the previous chapter I described characteristics of a conventional understanding of the utopian and why I think we should reject it. Unlike the other traits mentioned there, however, I want to retain a notion also associated with traditional utopian thinking yet develop it in a particular manner. This is, in general, the function of the utopian. In particular, I want to argue that the principal function of the utopian is to interrupt us and reveal those impulses that have been hidden. It is this disruptive element, I will suggest, that enables us to name such encounters "utopian." At its best, the utopian, as the arm of critique potentially empowers us to call into question an order that has become untenable. In this way, the utopian is indispensable in its ability to unveil hidden potentialities that have otherwise been blocked by systems that have failed. The interruptive element of the utopian, then, can be said to be that instant which opens to us the inventive nature of the utopian as it brings together a variety of components (literary, social, political, religious, etc) to produce alternative modes of thinking and acting. The disruptive element is central because it "introduces imaginative variations on the topics of society, power, government, family, religion...." (Ricoeur, 1986: 16). From Plato to contemporary works, then, the utopian at its best is the "*imaginaire* of rupture," which enables us to remain critical "of the powers that be out of fidelity to an 'elsewhere,' to a society that is "not yet," a function that characterizes all emancipatory work (Kearney, 1984: 29).

Let me state clearly in these introductory remarks that what the interruptive capacity of the utopian represents is *not* some ideal state we either aim at or seek to perfect. In this regard, I retain the function of the utopian without the necessary entailments of form or content. Likewise, it is not about the *process* of the utopian coming into actuality. Both of these positions, in some way, retain either conventional notions of the utopian that are no longer viable (the former), or they presuppose an old-style Aristotelian ontological framework where every possibility strives to become actualized (the latter). Instead of interruption referring to possibility becoming actualized through an emphasis on the process, it instead refers to the unearthing of *unhidden potential* that is brought by interruption.[1] This difference from what I am developing is a key one, namely, that potential and possibility reflect two different ways of conceptualizing the work of the utopian itself. Those who substitute the process of the utopian with the move toward stasis in traditional models, still remain within a framework that characterizes both positions. Such emphasis on the process over against the more stasis-oriented notions often claims to be progressive, but is still, at best, a reactionary position and, I want to claim, an inversion of the same it rejects. To highlight the disruptive element is to recognize that the utopian, at its best, is *not* a version of the same but is instead a recognition of the deadlock created by the very coordinates of (utopian) thought itself. As a result, the interruptive capacity of the utopian is a possible *break* from the deadlock that is constituted by conventional utopian thought and its progressive counterpart with the emphasis on process. Let me put this slightly differently. If one emphasizes the process of the utopian, and this kind of thinking is dictated by and takes place *within* the coordinates defined by conventional utopian thinking itself (i.e., as moving toward a state of perfection and so forth), the language of process is itself dictated by these very coordinates, which renders a notion of the utopian that is thought to be radically different as a moment within the same. As a result, radical thought is not radical at all, but is itself a reactionary stance. This is why, in my project, I am attempting to think the utopian outside of these coordinates, which is why phenomenology and hermeneutics are not necessarily those that come to mind when one thinks of the utopian, but which are precisely in my estimation where we can reach to break the coordinates of thinking about the utopian that have created a deadlock that amounts to irrelevancy.

In a second and related way, interruption indicates possible scenarios tied to the "what-if" of the imaginative work of the utopian.

The utopian as an interruption is the "what-if" in Drucilla Cornell's description of the utopian as an opening to a threshold mentioned in the previous chapter. For my purposes, I want to link this imaginative work of the "what-if" with the disruptive force of the utopian and highlight the following. The interruptive "what if" is:

1. An awareness of the place of the contingent and fragile in approaching the utopian. It is a place within our embodied history where, through an interruption the utopian potential is revealed. The "what-if" is not an external place beyond history, but a way of indicating how the utopian, if it is to become for us a potential, does so in a realistic manner with our lives.

2. A reminder of the *universal emancipatory* impetus of the utopian. Even though our particularities shape the utopian, the utopian, at its disruptive best, reminds us of the work of universal liberation that is potentially possessed by all, yet incapable of being lived because of circumstances, structures so on.

3. Is the demand to seize a moment that, perhaps in a flash, is presented as a potentially different way to live ethically and politically, a moment that is more likely flawed yet nonetheless viable and, if we are honest, may recede as quickly as it appears.

In light of this discussion maybe it is better to speak of the utopian as an *ad-vent* instead of an *event*. For the utopian as an event suggests to me that it is something we can master, something *we* can produce, an unfamiliar that can be *made* familiar.[2] This does not capture the potency of the utopian. Rather, to speak of the utopian as an *ad-vent* is to suggest that it cannot readily be made into an event, where this means mastering its content, form and even its function. The idea of an advent crystallizes this element insofar as the utopian encounter shatters our given understandings of society and always remains beyond actualization (both conceptually and practically) and instead reflects the potential that the encounter flashes before us. In this way, we could say that instead of being a possibility that can become actual, the utopian is impossible by which I mean the following.

The hoping and dreaming that is part and parcel of any utopian politics is not so much for the possible that becomes actual, as it is a passion for the *impossible*.[3] First off you should not hear me saying that the utopian is absolutely absolute, infinitely other, senseless and incoherent. To say that would make the utopian in this form yet another state toward which we are moving. Furthermore, it would render the utopian unrealistic. Both of these are, as I have already suggested, components of the conventional view that I reject. It is, instead, a *passion* for the impossible, which is to say that the interruption of the utopian occurrence drives us, provokes us, and keeps open the encounter of such thought. Our passion or drive for that which we lack is an impossibility; an impossibility that arises in pathos which at once births a longing for that which we cannot see clearly but that which nevertheless disturbs us to the existential bone. To speak of the utopian as impossible, then, is always to keep open the "not-yet" of the active imagination. The impossibility of the utopian is also a way of characterizing its power of solicitation, a solicitation that always shocks our system, jars our dreams of perfection, and opens those crevices of determination so that we can move toward new potentialities. So, the impossibility of the utopian is anything but a deferral of action. Rather, we could say, following Merleau-Ponty, whose work I will discuss more closely in the following chapters, that the impossibility of the utopian is an active transcendence that impels us toward response, what in Chapter Five I will refer to as the interpretive demand of the utopian. What is important to note here is that the newness in thought, the interruption, is dialectically intertwined with newness in action. Let me borrow a line from Derrida to elaborate this idea. He says: "Go there where you cannot go, to the impossible, that is at bottom the only way of going or coming. To go there where it is possible, that is not to surrender, rather, it is to be there already and to be paralyzed in the in-decision of the non-event" (Derrida, 1995: 75).

To give of yourself, to surrender as Derrida says is to set out passionately for that which has shattered your familiarity and go where you cannot go. That is to say, the utopian gets us moving. Anything less is to remain stuck in place with the same. Going where you cannot go,

like the offering of forgiveness when retribution is justified, going some-
where impossible, like releasing a people from their past—not letting
them forget it but forgiving them—these are the impossible potentialities that are brought with the advent of the utopian. This impossibility,
these impossible actions are what movement toward new openings is
really all about. All else is pseudo-motion, paralysis, or as Derrida says
non-event. The utopian operates on such a plane by moving us toward
an engagement with both impossible thought and action on behalf of
the utopian to the world. This is why, as I will argue later, the element
that emerges from this idea is that of being a responsible witness to the
utopian. As that which is impossible it is that which we desire the most,
above all, and that which we love (*Eros*) to the point that it can drive
us mad (*pathos*). This, then, is the double-sided nature of the utopian:
that which drives us toward transformation can likewise drive us mad,
pathologically.

In the end, perhaps I can say it best like this. Impossibility signifies our erotic striving that is *not* toward some final goal; instead it is a
striving toward that which, though often glimpsed, is never completely
attainable. Thus, to stress the utopian as the impossibility brought on
by the advent of disruption is to place emphasis on its ability to keep
open the space of critique and acknowledge that the utopian cannot
bring about a perfect state, fixed for all times, where thought and action
completely cease to exist or become actualized.

It should be clearer from the above discussion how the notion
of the utopian as advent is crucial to my understanding. The *advent*
shocks, shatters, and transforms us into *ad-venturing* beings, beings
who venture towards (ad) something of which we are not sure, though
we are with it, or it is elusively with us—yet not in the sense that it can
be mastered. And I want to add, while the occurrence for the utopian
is individual—structured by our lived bodily experience (as we will see
in the next chapter)—it by no means takes place in isolation. We are
intertwined with others in our utopian ad-ventures.

The interruptive ad-vent of the utopian, then, is an "astonishing"
moment in our lives, one that happens (perhaps) only on rare occa-
sions. I use "astonishing" intentionally to invoke one of Plato's uses

of θαυμάζειν. θαυμάζειν is the lot of the philosopher in general but the utopian in particular, if we are to believe Plato. θαυμάζειν is most often translated as "wonder," that phrase we all love to use when we witness to the attraction of *philosophia*. However, in addition to wonder, *astonishment* is an equally good translation.[4] Astonishment and ad-vent. Ways to describe the interruptive power of the utopian. To be astonished is, after all, to be rocked back on one's heels by something of which we do not quite know the exact content. There is a shock in this astonishment; nothing short of a rupture that takes our breath away. In this interruptive moment we find ourselves illuminated by a sudden surge of something we cannot take hold of, something that, perhaps though I am not sure, may not be mediated. We can prepare for advents, though we never know when they come or even if they have. My point is that the interruption is an astonishing opening, which we cannot produce our *selves*. This is a moment that derives its understanding, or structure, from our lived bodily existence.

The rupture that shatters our complacency in the world does not paralyze us. Rather, as I have been saying, it drives us—erotically—toward that which has wrenched us out of our habitual familiarity with the things of the world. Its impossibility impassions us. And, as we all know in these times, such ruptures are painful, which recalls for us Plato's other use of θαυμάζειν, *pathos*. For all of the astonishment and wonder that the utopian moment brings, as we know when wrestling with a newness we know little about it also brings suffering. Accordingly, the ad-venture of the utopian means for us that in our actions on behalf of transformation there will be an undergoing driven by the desire for that which we lack, that risks itself in attempting to make sense of that which exceeds our grasp and that which cannot finally be translated into rational blueprints that can order all of society. In addition, it will mean we risk ourselves for that which has shattered our complacency.

Take, for instance, the following remark made by Slavoj Žižek apropos Lenin. Žižek writes:

> [I]n a genuine revolutionary breakthrough, the utopian future
> is neither simply fully realized, present, nor simply evoked as a

distant promise which justifies violence—it is rather as if, in a unique suspension of temporality, in the short circuit between the present and the future, we are—as if by Grace—briefly allowed to act *as if* the utopian future is (not yet fully here, but) already at hand, there to be seized (Žižek, 2002: 259).

In addition to the way Žižek intimates what I have been arguing for, his introduction of grace as a disruptive force is helpful. This language, albeit owing much to a theological tradition, can be understood as a moment that encapsulates the way the utopian breaks in to offer the alternative that is there in the encounter. Alain Badiou has written similarly on what can be described as the utopian moment of grace found in the Apostle Paul. In particular, Badiou writes that grace is "what comes upon us in the caesura of the law. It is pure and simple an *encounter*" (Badiou, 2008: 106). As with Žižek, Badiou's claim is significant because, on the one hand, it indicates the way an alternative (grace), relates always to the standard (law). On the other hand, it emphasizes what I here am calling the interruption of the utopian as an advent ("what comes upon us"). Taken together, Badiou's and Žižek's remarks help us to see that the interruptive work of the utopian (here grace) is both apart of the subject itself (its relation to the law), and that which comes to us as a challenge, potential and ultimately an interruption. What I want to do is explore this relation of grace and law through this interruptive lens of the utopian and, in doing so, reveal more precisely *how* the work of interruption might be understood. As with other chapters, I want to invoke work that does not immediately come to mind as utopian, but can nevertheless aid us in the task of thinking the utopian differently. In this case I refer to the work of cognitive linguistics.

Utilizing empirical research from cognitive science, cognitive linguistics has shown that metaphor is a basic structure of human understanding; that is to say, all of our major concepts are defined by systems of conceptual metaphors (Gibbs 1994, Johnson 1989; Lakoff 1990, Lakoff & Johnson, 1980). A conceptual metaphor, therefore, is a conceptual structure by which we understand and reason about a domain of one (the target domain) by means of knowledge drawn from a domain of a different kind (the source domain). A conceptual metaphor consists of a target, a source, and a mapping between them, the latter of which is illustrated by lines connecting components in the source domain with those in the target domain. What cognitive linguists are continually showing us, further, is that conceptual metaphors are a matter of thought and not simply a matter of language. Accordingly, a cognitive linguistic understanding of metaphor differs from the traditional understandings of metaphor that view it as, say, an ornament to or deviance in language (cf. Aristotle and Richard Rorty). Accordingly, I take this key insight of cognitive linguistics, the constitutive importance of conceptual metaphor, and describe not only how the economy of grace, particularly a Christian understanding, is structured by two fundamental conceptual metaphors: GRACE AS GIFT and MORAL ACCOUNTING. In particular, I will demonstrate how the former interrupts the latter in the way I have been suggesting is central to the work of the utopian.

In order to show how the economy of grace is structured by a conceptual metaphor of gift-giving, I later explore this conceptual metaphor relative to another conceptual metaphor, that of MORAL ACCOUNTING. There I will show two things. First, we cannot understand the GRACE AS GIFT metaphor independent of this MORAL ACCOUNTING metaphor because the MORAL ACCOUNTING metaphor enables us to read and think about particular gifts as being either deserved or not deserved, something fundamental to any understanding of grace. Second, only after we understand the economy of MORAL ACCOUNTING, and its relationship to the metaphor of GRACE AS GIFT, can we see how the GRACE AS GIFT economy challenges and consequently ruptures the MORAL ACCOUNTING metaphorical system.

What I explicitly claim, therefore, is that the GRACE AS GIFT metaphor exists within the MORAL ACCOUNTING metaphor. If this is so, then what is initially viewed as a radical concept, grace, is in fact a concept that relies on a conceptual metaphor that pervades Western thought. Furthermore, in terms of the utopian, once we become cognizant of the MORAL ACCOUNTING metaphor, we can then see more clearly how the GRACE AS GIFT metaphor interrupts the MORAL ACCOUNTING metaphor thereby revealing a potentially new way for living. Let us now turn to the specifics for understanding a cognitive analysis of GRACE AS GIFT.

The language of grace is used often. "There but for the grace of God go I," "She is a gracious person," "We are in his good graces." And we often think that acting graciously towards another is potentially an ideal way of relating. However, even though the concept of grace permeates our lives most of us are really unable to articulate what it means.

Mapping the Grace as Gift Metaphor

When we consider the biblical evidence for grace, what is revealed is a unified picture of the concept of grace. This is that of GRACE AS GIFT. What follows is an elaboration of the logic of the metaphor of GRACE AS GIFT, indicated by a mapping of the metaphor, which is then followed by a detailed analysis of the inference structure inherent in the mapping.

GIFT	GRACE
Gift	God's self
Giver	God
Receiver	Humanity
Motivation for the gift	Reunion
Accept gift	Accept God's gift of grace
Reject gift	Reject God's gift of grace
Undeserved/Unexpected gift	Justification in spite of sin
Responsibility for accepting/ rejecting gift	Responsibility for accepting/ rejecting God's gift of grace

Let us examine the inference structure of this mapping more carefully.

1.1 *The Gift of Grace*

Attempting to discern the gift of God's grace is difficult. Initially we most likely say that the gift is something like forgiveness, mercy, shalom or something similar. Stating that the gift of grace is one or more of these things does not, however, really explain what the gift is; these characteristics provide beginning points for further analysis. The gift of grace, therefore, seems to be that which is the precondition of "receiving" favor, mercy, forgiveness, etc.

I submit that the gift of grace is God's self-presence, or at least for Judaism the manifestation of God's will in Torah as a supreme act of grace. The issue of the presence of God as a gift is, to be sure, problematic and debatable. To say that the gift of God's grace is the presence of God is not to disagree that the gift is forgiveness or any other notion. My claim is that regardless of the concept chosen, other characteristics such as forgiveness or favor require God's presence. The purpose of saying that the gift of God's grace is God's presence is to show that God's presence is what is projected onto the target domain of grace whenever we activate the need for a gift in the source domain of giving. Let us look at some examples where this is the case.

Grace is often used to describe the relationship between the superior and the inferior such as a relationship between a King and a subject. The King does not have to communicate with the inferior person. However, the King decides either to make himself present or allow the inferior one into his presence and this is seen to have grace (favor) on the one with whom he communicates (2 Samuel, 14:22). Grace is used to describe the Yahweh's relationship to Israel. Yahweh reveals Yahweh's self to Moses. Moses leads the people from exile. The people of Israel become disgruntled and Moses wonders what Yahweh has in mind for him as Israel's leader. Moses, however, recalls that he has found grace (favor)in Yahweh's sight and says to Yahweh: "Now if I have found favor in your sight, show me your ways, so that I may know you and find favor in your sight. Consider too this nation is your people." Yahweh replies: "My presence will go with you, and I will give you rest" (Exodus, 33:13-14). The point here is that Yahweh's grace towards Moses and the people of Israel is the promise of Yahweh's continued presence.

God's presence as God's grace is also communicated by the Psalter when the poet wonders "Has God forgotten to be gracious? Has God in anger shut off compassion?" (Psalm, 77:9). God's absence is the lack of God's grace or self. Further, when the poet says "Turn to me and be gracious to me, for I am lonely and afflicted" (Psalm, 25:16), there is a cry for God to be present so that relief might take place and forgiveness brought about (v.17). In short, God gives something the poet needs, which is described as forgiveness and compassion. Forgiveness and compassion, however, presuppose the presence of God.

The grace of God enables the covenantal promise to be kept. In other words, God's presence is desired so that Israel might prosper. If Israel violates its covenant with God, however, then Israel risks being out of favor with God—out of God's presence. Therefore, when many of the writers indicate that the people of Israel have been handed over to other gods or other nations it is implied that the people of Israel have rejected God's presence by rejecting the commandments of God. For example:

> They (Israel) rejected all the commandments of the Lord their God [...] Therefore the Lord was very angry with Israel and removed them out of his sight: none was left but the tribe of Judah [...] The Lord rejected all the descendents of Israel; he punished them and gave them into the hand of plunderers, until he had banished them from his presence" (2 Kings, 17:16a, 18:20).

The same fate eventually happened to Judah, the Southern Kingdom, which abandoned the covenant with God and as a result was condemned to exile. God says to the prophet Jeremiah, "Therefore I will hurl you (Judah) out of this land into a land that neither you nor your ancestors have known, and there you shall serve other gods day and night, for I will give you no favor" (Jeremiah, 16:13). Because they have broken the covenant with God the people of Judah will be without the presence of God.

The Christian scriptures characterize the gift of grace more particularly as God's self-presence. Mary was told that she would give birth to Jesus. She was visited by an angel who said to her, "Greetings, you who are favored (graced). The Lord is with you" (Luke, 2:28). God's presence with Mary in the birth of Jesus is communicated as grace. God's self-presence is directly linked with the incarnation of Jesus. After Jesus' birth we are told that "the child grew and became strong, filled with wisdom; and the grace of God was upon him" (Luke, 2:40). In other words, God's presence was with Jesus (as is later illustrated by the descending of the dove at Jesus' baptism).

A predominant Christian claim is that God's self-revelation in Jesus provides humanity with a clear revelation of God. The incarnation, consequently, is viewed among other things as an act of grace. Thus, in the prologue to the Gospel of John, God, portrayed as Word, action and revelation, becomes fully present.

> And the Word became flesh and lived among us, and we have seen his glory, the glory of a father's only son, full of grace and truth. John testified to him and cried out: This was he of whom I said, "He who comes after me ranks ahead of me because he was before me." From his fullness we have all received, *grace upon grace*. The law indeed was given through Moses; grace and truth came through Jesus Christ. No one has ever seen God. It is God the only son, who is close to the father's heart, who has made him known' (John,1:14-18).

The writer of John communicates that Jesus is the revelation of God, and indicates as much by claiming that we have received the gift of God's "presence upon presence."

God's grace is also seen as a source of strength in times of persecution or difficulties. What is claimed, however, is that it is God's presence that provides strength. Paul tells us that he was afflicted with a "thorn in the flesh" and he prayed three times for it to be removed. The thorn was never removed. God's response to Paul's prayer was "My grace is sufficient for you, for my power is made perfect in weakness" (2Cor., 12:9). In other words, God's presence is that which will sustain Paul through his troubles. Likewise, God's presence also enables the message of the gospel to be carried on in a universal manner. As such, God's presence is viewed as God's grace upon those who have received God's empowerment. Only after the Apostles receive God's presence of the Holy Spirit were they able to preach with great power. As a result of this presence that "gave their testimony to the resurrection of the Lord Jesus, and great grace was upon them all" (Acts 4:33). What was on them? The presence of God in the form of the Holy Spirit.

There are two contemporary examples worth mentioning that also portray the gift of grace as God's self-presence. First Martin Marty defines grace as that concept which expresses the character of God.

> God had the freedom to remain unrelated; instead God was moved to create a universe, to situate humans in it, to move toward them [...]. God is love; whatever it means this reality suggests that God is moved by nothing other than that love to visit humans, bring them back to God, and restore them. This love, unmotivated and spontaneous [...] finds expression in grace. Grace, therefore, better than any other term, exemplifies the revelation of the divine character in action and the relation of the divine to human beings. The notion of pure grace as gift is as likely to be heard proclaimed in Catholic as in Protestant circles. (Marty, 1992: 210-211).

Leonardo Boff, a Roman Catholic liberation theologian, defines grace in the following manner.

> Grace signifies the presence of God in the world and in human beings. When God chooses to be present, the sick are made to be well, the fallen are raised up, the sinners are made just, the dead come back to life, the oppressed experience freedom, and despairing feel consolation and warm intimacy [...]. Grace is

the gift of the Father himself in Jesus Christ, the gratuitous
and merciful love of the Father and Christ which penetrates
human beings, liberating them, saving them from perdition, and
turning them into new creatures [...]. [The Apostle] Paul's use
of the word "grace" embodies concrete experience: God loved
me first, despite my sins, because he is good, benevolent, and
merciful. Paul feels graced by a gift, the gift of God himself in
Jesus Christ. Christ is grace: God present to us. This experience
of being surprised by an unexpected gift is what Paul expresses
with the word "grace" (Boff, 1979: 3: 49).

What these passages reveal is that the gift of grace relates to the self-
presence of God, whether in the law as the manifestation of the divine
will, or in the person of Jesus. Even though we do not normally talk
of the gift of grace as God's presence, what the inference pattern of
the metaphorical mapping reveals is that this conception is activated
automatically whenever we do speak of the gift of grace. To emphasize,
this is not to deny that the gift of grace is often conceptualized as
forgiveness, mercy, shalom, peace, happiness and so on. It is my
contention that as important as these concepts figure in our talk of
grace they all presuppose the presence of God.

1.2 *The Giver of the Gift*

Whenever a gift is given there is a giver. The giver can be someone
who is superior or inferior as indicated in the example of the relationship
between a King and a Subject. Regardless of one's position as the giver
of the gift, the logic of giving is such that when one gives something
to someone else, one discloses a part of him or herself to the receiver.
The giver does not have to know whether or not the other will accept
or reject the gift. When the gift is rejected, the giver, by extension is
also rejected. This same logic applies to the way we conceptualize God's
presence as gift. Can the giver be both the giver and the gift? Based
on the logic of giving the answer is yes. Insofar as we give a portion of
ourselves to someone whenever we give them a gift. The act of giving is
the act of disclosing one's self. Even if we give a gift we consider to be

a full manifestation of ourselves we are aware that one particular gift does not exhaust us; we will give other gifts.

There is, then, a certain risk to giving a gift. Following the logic of giving, which we map onto the way we conceptualize grace, God must have known that rejection was a possibility in giving God's self. This seems to be true for both the Christian and Jewish traditions. Many times the people of Israel rejected the law and by extension rejected the giver. The same is true for Christianity. The giver of the gift of self-presence was not accepted by all. If this had been the case, then there would have been no crucifixion. Nevertheless, God chose, in spite of the possibilities of rejection, to be present to humanity so that humanity might be given a further means to reconciliation.

1.3. Receiver of the Gift

Similarly, acceptance and rejection of a gift require a receiver. If the gift of grace is God's presence, and this gift can be both accepted and rejected, then to whom is the gift given? A Christian claim is that God's self-presence, specifically revealed in Jesus, is a gift available to all who will receive it (John, 1:12). The condition, however, is both to accept this message and follow him accordingly.

In sum, what the linguistic analysis reveals thus far is that the logic of giving enables us to reason about God's gift of self-presence as that which can be either accepted or rejected. If we accept the gift we accept a part of the one who gives the gift. Likewise, if we reject the gift we are saying in effect that we reject a part, or maybe even all, of the one who is represented in the gift. We can choose to accept God's self-presence or we can choose to reject God's presence. But why does God, in spite of the possibilities of rejection, decide to give God's self to humanity? To answer this we have to discuss the motivation for giving the gift.

1.4. Motivation for Giving the Gift

We give gifts for different reasons. We give gifts that are often viewed as silly and meaningless. We also give gifts that carry with them a deep and abiding meaning. Therefore, our motivations for giving gifts can range from embarrassing someone to symbolizing one's deep commitment to another. What is the motivation for God giving the gift?

The motivation for the giving of God's self could be characterized as reunion. The reunion is with God, ourselves, and others. If it is sin (both individual and social) that alienates us from God, ourselves, and others, then it is God's giving of God's self that reconciles us with God and provides the means by which we can be reconciled with ourselves and others. This claim, though interpreted differently, appears basic to the Christian faith. God's gift of grace removes the obstacles to a relationship between God and humans. Dorothee Sölle writes:

> If sin means separation, segregation, isolation and alienation, then grace is the reunion of the living with the origin of life— and thus precisely what God wills. It is simply the happiness of no longer being separated. The wish for reunion is one of the deepest human wishes, and it is precisely for that reason that separation is so destructive. To be with God means no longer to be separated (Sölle, 1990: 79).

God's gift of grace as a reunion with God is also a healing (as Paul Tillich says) of our "True Being." To be sure, sin is characterized in many ways. Generally speaking, however, sin has been portrayed exclusively in individual terms (e.g. pride). While this is certainly a way to speak of sin, other theologians have shown that to speak of sin as simply a matter of pride or some other particular trait is to risk universalizing a particular (usually male experience).

Liberation, African-American, and feminist theologians have challenged this universalizing of experience and shown that sin is not only individual (e.g. pride) but sin is also social (as with racism, sexism, etc). Individual alienation derives from a social dimension of sin, which diminishes each individual's capacity for self-actualization. How, then, does the motivation of God's gift of grace relate to this? The experience of the gift of grace is, as Judith Plaskow says, an experience of "turning" that has both individual and social implications both of which reveal the utopian potential. She writes:

> The woman who, having seen the non-being of social structures, feels herself a whole person is called upon to become the person she is in that moment. The discontinuity of the experience of wholeness with her previous development means that she must work slowly and painfully through the concrete changes her vision entails. Yet she cannot become a new person without working for her transformation of a society in which women and men are socialized into roles which prevent each sex from appropriating the important human qualities of the other. The need for and possibility of personal and social transformation is discerned in the context of community, and the continuing process of questioning, growth, and change remains collective and is aimed at the collective (Plaskow, 1980: 171-172).

What this component of our analysis reveals, then, is that the gift of God's self-presence as grace reunites us with God and by extension provides us with a means by which we can be united with our true being. Such reunification, or fellowship, can take the form of individual reunion from sins of pride or other individual sins. It can also be a reunification with one's self whereby one takes responsibility for becoming a self. Last, reunion can motivate us to overcome the social dimension of sin(s) where racism, sexism and all types of oppression contribute to individual alienation. In short, the motivation for God giving God's self, then, is a reunion and wholeness for all.

1.5. *Purpose of the Gift*

When we accept a gift our lives are potentially changed. To accept a gift we perceive as important means to adopt the responsibility and risk that goes with accepting the gift. The logic of giving yields the idea that there is a responsibility linked with accepting (and for that matter rejecting) a gift offered to us. This same logic of responsibility that we apply to accepting or rejecting gifts maps onto the way we conceptualize grace.

We either accept the gift of grace (God's self presence) or reject the gift and we accordingly accept or reject the responsibilities that go along with the gift. In other words, if we accept the gift we accept the privilege and responsibility that comes with the gift. Generally, for Christians to accept God's self-presence as a gift is to accept not only God's liberating message of salvation but to accept God's demand on us. In Chapter Five I will discuss this in terms of being a responsible witness to the utopian. To accept the gift of God's self-presence is to accept the responsibility of obedience to God. If we choose to accept the gift this means for Christians choosing obedience to the commands revealed in Jesus' life and teachings. This is intimated when Jesus says, "In any want to become my followers, let them deny themselves and take up their cross and follow me. For those who want to save their life will lose it, and those who lose their life for my sake, and for the sake of the gospel, will save it" (Mark, 8:34-35). The gift cost the life of God's only son or God's self, and as a result of accepting the gift, so this logic goes, it requires our lives. To emphasize, the gift of grace as only the gift of God's self-presence to humans and not God's demand for obedience is, what Dietrich Bonhoeffer called, "cheap grace" (Bonhoeffer, 1961: 35). If within this logic of the gift the idea of deserving and not deserving certain gifts occur, then what is needed is an understanding of how we conceptualize something as either deserved or undeserved. Here we begin to probe deeper into the GRACE AS GIFT conceptual metaphor, then other metaphors within which it operates, and the subsequent hidden potential that GRACE AS GIFT carries with it for ethical and political life.

1.6. *Deserving and Undeserving Gifts*

The logic of giving allows us to conceptualize the receiving of a gift that is either deserved or undeserved. This is the single most important aspect of the GRACE AS GIFT metaphor. As we saw above, we cannot only accept or reject gifts we can also receive gifts that we either do or do not deserve. We have all received gifts that we expected to get (e.g. a five-dollar gift given to us by a co-worker at a holiday party because of a five-dollar limit per gift). Moreover, we have all received gifts we did not expect to receive, gifts that took us by surprise (e.g. like receiving an "A" on a paper when we probably deserved a "B+"). Though this may be a trivial example, it illustrates my point that there have been times we all have received gifts that we did not expect. Additionally, some gifts are given in spite of our rejection. In this respect, if someone is determined for you to have a particular gift you cannot reject the gift. This maps onto our conceptualization of grace and leads us to ask, "Can one really reject the gift of the presence of God?"

In general, Christianity has claimed that one receives salvation when he or she accepts Jesus as Lord and Savior. In some traditions this claim has been interpreted to say that one receives the grace of God by, for example, accepting the sacraments. There have been traditions, however, that have claimed that no matter what, God's favor is "assured." I am thinking of two traditions: Calvinism and Universalism. Some understand the former to argue for divine election where God chooses those to be saved. Some understand the latter to be claiming that because God is love, God will allow everyone to be saved. I am not interested in evaluating the status of these interpretations. Rather, my point is that both conceptualize the gift of grace (here something like salvation) as something we receive and which is not invalidated by our actions.

This illustration reveals the following. Once we begin to reason and think of GRACE AS GIFT in terms of deserving and not deserving something, we activate another conceptual metaphor that is significant for understanding the economy of GRACE AS GIFT. In order to conceptualize what it is to receive something either deserved or undeserved we activate an economy based on a conceptual metaphor of MORAL ACCOUNTING. Below I will show how the GRACE AS GIFT schema interrupts the MORAL ACCOUNTING metaphor, but before we see how the logic of GRACE AS GIFT challenges this MORAL ACCOUNTING METAPHOR, we must first understand what is meant by the MORAL ACCOUNTING system.

The Moral Accounting Metaphor

The MORAL ACCOUNTING metaphor structures the way we specify certain procedures to establish both what we owe and what someone else owes under specific situations. The MORAL ACCOUNTING metaphor enables us to conceptualize a system where we do something for someone else and they in turn owe us something in return (or vice versa). With the MORAL ACCOUNTING metaphor we conceptualize well being as wealth. That is, we understand an increase in one's well being as financial gain. Therefore, doing something good to another increases her or his well being. The good act or moral act is understood via metaphor as a commodity that is given to another for the purpose of increase in well being. The opposite is true as well. We understand a decrease in one's well being as a loss. So, that which benefits is a profit; that which harms is a loss. Mark Johnson, who has spent a great deal of effort analyzing the MORAL ACCOUNTING metaphor, summarizes this in the following way.

> Giving someone something good is giving him a valuable commodity (or its monetary equivalent), which, by the MORAL ACCOUNTING metaphor, amounts to increasing his well-being. Giving someone something bad is a more complex notion—it amounts to harming her in some way, or decreasing her well being. Decreasing her well being is understood as taking a valuable commodity (or monetary equivalent) from her. What is needed to work out the precise details of this metaphorical conception is an arithmetical notion of negative values. If giving someone something good is giving him a commodity of positive value, then giving him something bad is giving him a commodity with a negative value. The negative value amounts to taking something of positive value away from the other person, and so reducing her well being (Johnson, 1993: 47).

Our knowledge of morality is structured in terms of economic transactions that map on to the way we understand moral obligations to others and their corresponding responsibilities. Consequently, moral acts are conceptualized in terms of financial transactions. There are moral acts (credits) and immoral (or sinful) acts (debits). And whereas financial books must be balanced, so must the moral books. This understanding of moral credits and debits along with the need for balanced moral books (understood metaphorically) enables us to conceptualize receiving something that is deserved and undeserved. If I do something good to someone, I build up moral credit. If, however, I do something bad to someone, they deserve restitution so that the books are balanced in the end. The mapping for the MORAL ACCOUNTING metaphor, in this light, can be understood as follows.[5]

Commodity Transaction	Moral interaction
Objects, Commodities	Deeds (actions), states
Utility or Value of objects	Moral worth of actions
Wealth	Well Being
Accumulation of goods	Increase in Well Being
Profitable =causing increase of wealth	Moral (godly) =causing increase in well-being
Unprofitable= causing decrease in wealth	Immoral (sinful)=causing decrease in well-being
Money (as surrogate for goods)	Well Being
Giving/taking money or commodities	Performing godly/sinful deeds
Account of transactions	Moral account
Balance of account	Moral balance of deeds
Debt	Moral debt=owing something good to God or another
Credit	Moral credit= others owe you something good/God's blessing
Fair exchange/payment	Justice

Based on what we have seen thus far, what becomes clearer is that we inherit this MORAL ACCOUNTING whenever we conceptualize grace. Consider the following illustration.

In many Christian traditions to break God's law is to risk the wrath of God. To ensure justice everyone must follow the laws that God has provided (whether these are construed as the Ten Commandments in particular or more broadly as the teaching of Jesus).[6] These laws, as it were, have a purpose, namely, to ensure that people do what God wants. To follow that law, therefore, is, among other things, to "do the will of God." Accordingly, when the laws are broken injustice occurs and there is a need to balance the books so that justice can prevail. There is retribution for breaking the laws. Often in Christianity, whether we disagree or not, the punishments are thought to be brought about by God, which are necessary in order to balance the (moral) books. Certain biblical phrases reveal this MORAL ACCOUNTING metaphor and the need to have balanced (moral) books. One of the most familiar phrases is "An eye-for-an-eye and a tooth-for-a-tooth." This phrase indicates the means by which we are to attain balanced (moral) books. Whether we deem this idea as repulsive is not the point here. In fact, as we will see, the GRACE AS GIFT metaphor shows the limitations of this idea and shatters the "eye-for-an-eye" schema.

Let me summarize what this analysis yields. The linguistic evidence suggests that the bad (sinful) acts are seen as debits, good (moral) acts are seen as credits. Doing good acts is often thought to accumulate in such a fashion as to be able to withstand severe retribution for the sinful acts we do. For example, we do a lot of little good things so that when we do one big bad thing we still have enough (moral) credit on our side of the ledger that prevents something being taken from us to balance out our bad act. To continue to do sinful acts, however, is inevitably to produce an imbalance in the moral books. What is needed, then, is a way to balance the books again. This is precisely why God is often conceived as some kind of a cosmic moral accountant. God keeps the moral books balanced by doing whatever is necessary. God curses humanity because of humanity's persistent sinful ways. Likewise, when humanity is blessed by God, humanity is thought to be "morally right" with God. No story illustrates the pervasiveness of the MORAL ACCOUNTING metaphor better than that of Job.

Job's friends tell him that his sin has caused his suffering. On their account, God's retribution is to take away all that is precious to Job. This balances out Job's sinful action. In effect, Job's friends think that Job's moral credit (metaphorically understood) is bad. Job, however, knows that he has done nothing wrong (we are told as much as well). Thus, he feels justified in protesting loudly to God, asking why he should receive such suffering.

We are told that Job was a righteous man. Yet when Job loses everything he is told by his friends that he must have done something bad (sinful) to bring about this suffering. Now, most of us would no doubt argue that Job's friends were wrong in their assessment of Job's character and God's relating to humanity. However, Job's friend Eliphaz asks Job why he is dismayed at his own trouble and their response to it, thereby suggesting that theirs is a common way of reasoning and thinking about such matters. Eliphaz reminds Job:

> Is not your fear of God your confidence, and the integrity of your ways your hope? Think now, who that was innocent ever perished? Or where were the upright cut off? As I have seen, those who plough iniquity and sow trouble reap the same. By the breath of God they perish, and by the blast of his anger they are consumed. The roar of the lion, the voice of the fierce lion, and the teeth of the young lions are broken. The strong lion perishes for lack of prey, and the whelps of the lioness are scattered (Job, 4:6-11).

Norman Habel provides a helpful commentary regarding the tradition revealed in this passage, along with the way this tradition conceived of such matters. He writes:

> [The wisdom tradition focuses] forcibly on the moral character of God. God is honorable, they [Job's friends] argue, operating strictly according to the divine principles of cosmic and moral order established from the beginning. Where humans are

righteous, God blesses them; where they are wicked God chastises, afflicts, or, in the last resort, destroys them. The God of the friends is not a God who acts or interferes but a God who reacts. The pattern of the universe, with is inbuilt moral code, is already determined. Justice is a guaranteed system of reward and retribution, of God reacting to the good or ill that mortals do (Habel, 1992: 26-27).

This quote provides a synopsis of the cognitive make-up of the friends of Job. It is safe to assume, further, that they were not the only ones who thought in this fashion. This way of thinking (whether we agree or disagree with it is not the point here) is carried over into the Christian scriptures when Jesus is asked upon seeing a man born blind "Who sinned, this man or his parents?" (John, 9). Clearly, as with Job's friends, sin and disability are linked in the minds of the questioners. Jesus, like Job before him, interrupts this line of thought.

My point here is that the story of Job, along with the blind man and numerous other stories in both testaments, exemplifies the economy of MORAL ACCOUNTING because it reveals a desire on the part of many (if not most) for the (moral) books to be balanced (Job should confess his sin so that God will once again bless him, read: Job's debits outweigh his credits). As his friends suggest, Job's own bad (sinful) acts are negative acts that upset the (moral) books. As such, his suffering exists to re-establish a (moral) balance. More importantly, what is intimated in this line of thinking is that God is well within God's right to take whatever is needed from Job because Job has caused an imbalance in the moral books.

The story of Job is only one of many illustrations of how the MORAL ACCOUNTING metaphor structures our understanding of moral credits and debits with the need for moral balance. A more contemporary example might be something like the more good (godly) acts one does on earth the more one receives in heaven. Let me use a personal example. I recall as a youth that parishioners made distinctions between ministers and lay Christians. It was believed and taught that if we had "taken Jesus as our Lord and Savior" we would all receive a "crown of jewels" when we died and entered heaven. However, it was assumed that ministers would "get more jewels in their crowns" by virtue of the fact that they had preached and consequently converted more believers than the average lay person. This might seem like an unbelievable example but it is a variation, perhaps an extreme one, of the MORAL ACCOUNTING metaphor with its logic of moral credit and debits and balanced books. The point is that whether for Job's friends, Jesus' interlocutors, or twenty-first century Christians in this case, the MORAL ACCOUNTING metaphor is a deep conceptual metaphor that allows us to reason and think about the receiving of deserved or undeserved gifts.

I want to return to my example of Calvinism and Universalism. These two traditions of Christianity have been cause for heated debate. Rightly or wrongly, the doctrine of predestination, often associated with Calvinism, and a doctrine of an all-loving God incapable of "sending anyone to hell," often associated with the tradition of Universalism, are controversial. Besides the fact that both traditions are complex and nuanced in their understanding of these ideas, I suggest, in light of the above discussion, that one reason many people find these traditions provoking or disagreeable is because of the embeddedness of the widely shared MORAL ACCOUNTING metaphor in Western thought in general and Western Christianity in particular. Once we understand more clearly the logic of MORAL ACCOUNTING we can see that one reason that both Calvinism and Universalism cause so much debate is precisely because they, like Job above, question and even reject the fundamental entailments of the MORAL ACCOUNTING system of debits and credits that pervade our understanding.

Two important ideas are revealed in the above juxtaposition between the MORAL ACCOUNTING and GRACE AS GIFT metaphors. First, the GRACE AS GIFT conceptual metaphor relies on and derives from the pervasive MORAL ACCOUNTING metaphorical system, especially when we begin to conceive of deserving and not deserving certain gifts. Second, since the MORAL ACCOUNTING metaphor provides the framework out of which we reason about grace, our conceptualization of grace, while being radical in that it allows for the moral books to be balanced even when we can not balance them ourselves, relies on a metaphorical system already present, a system that hides the potentiality of an alternative way of thinking and living. Does this mean, then, that the economy of grace is such that it only gradually emerges from the MORAL ACCOUNTING metaphor?

To say that the GRACE AS GIFT metaphor appears within an already existing framework does not mean it does not *radically interrupt* the logic of MORAL ACCOUNTING. And here is where I would say that the GRACE AS GIFT metaphor exhibits the emancipatory potential of the utopian. The GRACE AS GIFT metaphor coalesces in such a manner that we see something that is counter to the logic of MORAL ACCOUNTING we are shocked at his or her actions because her or she acted outside the entailments of MORAL ACCOUNTING. As an occurrence for interruption the GRACE AS GIFT metaphor offers a new potential for being-together in the world, a utopian potentiality. My point is that even though the GRACE AS GIFT metaphor does challenge the MORAL ACCOUNTING framework, as Job challenged his friends, the GRACE AS GIFT metaphor is understood always relative to the background of the MORAL ACCOUNTING system and cannot be completely understood apart from it. Two things, then, can be said about this.

First, we cannot just set aside the economy of MORAL ACCOUNTING in favor of the GRACE AS GIFT, no matter how much we despise the former (as exemplified in Job's friends and Jesus' interlocutors). To do so is an illusion. We can, however, interrupt this dominant way of conceptualizing the deserving and undeserving of gifts, much like Job did to his friends. Second, the economies of GRACE AS GIFT and MORAL ACCOUNTING have to be understood relative to one another. It is only when we analyze and interrogate the MORAL ACCOUNTING metaphor can we see new possibilities for relating to each other in new and productive ways. In the final chapter, I will return in a slightly different way to the theme of this chapter by showing how the South African Truth and Reconciliation Commission (TRC) enacts this kind of interruption and unearths the utopian potential in its work, one based on forgiveness. For now, it is enough to say that, to be sure, there are those who want revenge or retribution for criminal participation in apartheid. However, the TRC attempts a new venture in healing and reconciliation by employing a form of GRACE AS GIFT metaphor by offering forgiveness as a gift to those who ask for it. It is a risk, as we have seen, but the rewards of this act of interruption are even greater for South Africa and the rest of us who deal with the past acts of atrocity.

We have, then, come full circle in this chapter. I began by claiming that the most important element of the utopian is its power to interrupt our most cherished ideas. We have seen how this is this case in the preceding discussion of grace. In particular, we were able to see how the interruption reveals not only an alternative potential for GRACE AS GIFT, but also the pervasiveness of the MORAL ACCOUNTING metaphor that tends to cover the hidden potential GRACE AS GIFT has for ethical and political life. We saw, in short, the utopian impulse at its best in the analysis above. Moreover, as with the example of Job, we began to see something hinted at in earlier sections of this chapter. This is the way that the demand that things be different, GRACE AS GIFT, emerge not from some abstract and disconnected account of grace itself, but rather from the way GRACE AS GIFT exists within the confines of our lived bodily existence in general and with the MORAL ACCOUNTING metaphor in particular. In this light, finally, we can raise in an initial way the question that will be the focus of the following chapter. This is the question of the relationship between the utopian and the embodied existence that, as I claim above, provides the framework from which the interruption comes. What I develop in the next chapter, therefore, is the bodily element of the utopian.

Chapter Three:

Forever Apart: The Bodily Element of the Utopian

To frame the argument in this chapter I want to begin with a claim made by Simon Critchley in his introductory essay for *A Companion to Continental Philosophy*. He writes that a "feature common to many philosophers in the Continental tradition" is the "*utopian* demand that things be otherwise" (Critchley, 1998a: 10, emphasis in original). His remark is unusual in two regards, both of which connect Continental philosophy (explicitly) and phenomenology and hermeneutics (implicitly) with being utopian.

His comment is uncommon first, because of the range of thinkers it appears to include. I say "appears" because he claims that *many* Continental philosophers exhibit this commitment to the utopian and that *the* Continental tradition itself is utopian. There would be virtually no disagreement that such a claim would apply to *some* movements within Continental philosophy. But *many*? There is little doubt, for example, that critical theory is a utopian movement within Continental philosophy and that this utopian dimension is one way of distinguishing critical theory from other traditions. The more modest claim, however, is not Critchley's. His pronouncement that the utopian is "common to many philosophers in the Continental tradition" is certainly stronger. Herein lies both more support for my interest in the utopian and, admittedly, its challenge.

To be sure, one could easily answer by saying phenomenologists are exceptions to Critchley's claim. Doing so, however, would in effect dismiss what is arguably *the* most dominant movement in Continental philosophy; a movement, both in its historically narrow formulations and its broader use by many of its contemporary practitioners that is often considered synonymous with "Continental philosophy."[1] Additionally, responding in this manner would call into question Critchley's claim that *many* in the Continental tradition are utopian, especially where the many either directly reflect a commitment to phenomenology or work in its shadow (an argument, for example, that one could make of deconstruction). My claim, however, is that phenomenology understood appropriately *is* a tradition that can and should be worthy of the label "utopian," and is why I agree with Critchley's claims. However, if Critchley (and my own project by extension) is to be taken seriously then some account of phenomenology should be given that demonstrates how it can be legitimately understood as utopian.[2] My aim in this chapter is to turn to this task and begin by offering an account of how Maurice Merleau-Ponty's phenomenology in particular provides a framework for beginning to think of phenomenology as utopian. Before I turn to the specifics of how this is the case, I want to point out another reason how Critchley's claim is startling.

His claim, second, is audacious for the way it makes a commitment to the utopian a *distinct* mark of Continental philosophy, and here implying strongly that *all* orientations in Continental philosophy are utopian (phenomenology and hermeneutics) and not just those that are self-described as utopian within this tradition (Critical Social Theory, for instance). In addition to the utopian, however, he mentions two other characteristics of this tradition that certainly extend to and emerge from phenomenology, qualities that many would point to in claiming that phenomenology and hermeneutics are *not* utopian. The other qualities mentioned are the radical finitude of the human subject and the thoroughly contingent or created character of human experience (Critchley, 1998a: 10). Given these two additional traits, it does not take much to see how his claim that the utopian is a "feature common to many philosophers in the Continental tradition" is bold if not downright contradictory. How, in the light of these other characteristics can the utopian be a *definitive* trait of Continental philosophy when the other two aspects suggest qualities that appear to be contrary? I say "appear to be contrary" for the following reason. These other characteristics, finitude and contingency, could perhaps more easily demonstrate how the utopian is *uncommon* to most Continental thinkers, especially those aligned with phenomenology.

Put differently, the trait that Critchley highlights as a decisive mark of Continental philosophy is one that is arguably considered a prominent enemy of contemporary philosophy in general, but especially Continental philosophy. Whereas many would claim that the utopian signals an interest in future projections that are naïve and ultimately irrelevant to our present situations, contemporary Continental philosophers are overwhelmingly concerned with philosophical issues pertinent to our present conditions, issues falling under the umbrellas of difference and otherness. Thus, the argument might go, since the utopian is a naïve projection of a world beyond our own, such a form of thinking ultimately *opposes* our finitude and contingency. With this view of the utopian one could easily make the case that to the degree that Continental philosophy relates to the utopian, it does so in a stance of *dis-engagement*. Let me elaborate.

When the word "utopian" appears on the pages of many Continental works in particular the utopian is most often, though certainly not always, assumed to be that kind of thinking against which a particular trajectory of thought is opposed (usually that of the author).[3] The understanding of the utopian operative in these cases is what I described in Chapter One as conventional (cf. Critchley, 1998b: 29). Recall how such a view is one where the utopian is synonymous with naïve, and static projections of the future that lie beyond our particular situations. In the frequent cases where the utopian is mentioned, the attending presumption is that the utopian is simply a cloak that hides the grand, over-arching, and totalizing metaphysics that has infected Western philosophy. Accordingly, the references to the utopian in many works of Continental philosophy, either explicitly or tacitly, suggest that as good Continental thinkers concerned with difference, otherness, finitude and contingency, we should either be suspicious of the utopian or reject it altogether for its irrelevancy at best, and its violent tendencies at worst. Specific support for this claim can be found in the following works of two prominent Continental philosophers, Jacques Derrida and Luce Irigaray.

First, with regards to democracy Derrida writes that we "always propose to speak of democracy *to come*, not of a *future* democracy or the future present, not even of a regulative idea, in the Kantian sense, or of a utopia—at least to the extent that their inaccessibility would still retain the temporal form of a *future present*, of a future modality of the *living present*" (Derrida, 1994: 64-65). Second, Irigaray states, " I am...a political militant for the impossible, *which is not to say a utopian*. Rather I want what is yet to be as the only possibility of a future" (Irigaray, 1996: 10, emphasis added). This is the extent to which they discuss the utopian (at least in these texts), yet it is enough to make my point that neither Derrida nor Irigaray says *what* they mean by the utopian, but their use of the term betrays what I have called a conventional understanding. For Derrida, the utopian is that form of thinking which lies beyond even a regulative ideal, Kantian or otherwise, where the future present becomes a modality or complete actuality of the living present. It is why he can conclude that the "here-now indicates that [political action] is not simply a question of utopia" (Derrida, 2002: 180).

Irigaray reflects a similar assumption. She opposes the militant to the utopian and suggests strongly that to be utopian is to be in favor of a future *possibility* that *is*, where we can only assume that *is* here means the possible future of the utopian completely actualized. In contrast, her own understanding of political militancy remains open to the future possibility that is always "yet to be," which is to say always becoming and never completely actualized. What is plain in both thinkers' remarks is that the utopian signifies for them a form of thought and practice from which good political activists should distance themselves. More importantly for my concerns, both thinkers clearly assume an understanding of the utopian that is otherworldly, unable to contribute to present political practices (democratic or militant), a form of thinking that privileges future actualization over future presence, and the kind of thinking that is problematic and violent. It is no surprise that they disassociate their own projects from anything utopian because, among other things, the utopian on their (conventional) understanding opposes our situations that are both finite and contingent. Their writing, in the end, certainly demonstrates how the utopian is common to Continental thinkers (both of whom owe much to phenomenology), just *not* in the way Critchley suggests.

One can begin to see, then, that making the argument that phenomenology in particular is a utopian tradition could be challenging and one perhaps better left alone. It is, however, an argument that can and should be made and one I want to advance in this chapter. My claim, which can now be stated clearer, is that phenomenology, particularly Merleau-Pontian phenomenology, offers a way to think the utopian in a non-conventional way that is different from the understanding assumed by Derrida, Irigaray, and many others. The key to my argument, it should be clearer now, turns on how we understand the notion of the utopian. As I proceed I will make a distinction between the conventional view of the utopian assumed by thinkers like Derrida and Irigaray and my non-conventional view of the utopian initiated in the previous two chapters. The element I want to develop here in terms of Maurice Merleau-Ponty's early work is that of embodiment and lived bodily existence (terms I distinguish below). Over thirty years ago Northrop Frye wrote the following:

> New utopias would have to derive their form from the shifting and dissolving movement of society that is gradually replacing the fixed locations of life. They would not be rational cities evolved by a philosopher's dialectic; *they would be rooted in the body* as well as in the mind, in the unconscious as well as the conscious, in forests and deserts as well as highways and buildings, in bed as in the symposium (Frye, 1966: 49, emphasis added).

Just what this might entail, Frye does not say. It is the aim of this chapter, therefore, to offer one philosophical response that takes up Frye's claim. I suggest that it is Merleau-Ponty who best equips us for the task of thinking about what it might mean to make the statement, suggested by my title, that utopian thinking is rooted in the body. Keeping in mind in previous chapters, I suggest that because he is not typically thought of as a utopian thinker, Merleau-Ponty is in a position to transform our thinking about the utopian itself. As one who through his explorations of embodiment reveals its transformative capacities, Merleau-Pontian phenomenology enables us to retrieve thought on the order of lived bodily experience that opens us to new potentialities. If, however, one possesses a conventional understanding of utopian thought as I discussed in Chapter One, then Merleau-Ponty will simply be viewed as anti-utopian insofar as he problematizes thought that seeks complete unity. It is at this point that I am critical of interpreters who claim he should *not* be thought of as a utopian thinker. To make such a claim, it should be clear from what I have already said, is to presuppose the traditional understanding of the utopian I reject.[4]

As this chapter will make clearer, Merleau-Ponty allows us to see the following. First, he enables us to see that utopian thought—like all thought—has its roots in embodiment. Second, his philosophy of the body, augmented at key points, reveals how the body interrupts those aspects of our tradition that inevitably confine, degrade and dehumanize us. Said in more political terms, Merleau-Ponty helps us to view lived bodily experience as the site whereby unlimited and diverse realities, which have gone unnoticed, are brought into focus and are capable of constructing new alternatives. But instead of constructing these alternatives in the name of dis-embodied principles, the inventive possibilities emerge in and through the active transcendence, or active engagement of one's lived bodily experience. This bodily basis for such thought *is* utopian and is why Merleau-Ponty's statement that "the *future* is only probable, but it is not an empty zone in which we can construct gratuitous projects; it is sketched before us like the beginning of the day's end, *and its outline is ourselves*," is an important one that serves as a guide for the argument that follows (Merleau-Ponty, 1969: 95, emphasis added).

What we will see as we proceed by examining the structures of embodiment is the following. First, our bodily existence is at once rooted in lived experience and at the same time moves out toward the world in action. Second, this is an understanding of the body that is organized and able to project certain aims that open us onto the world to what can rightly be called utopian potentialities. Finally, as an act of embodiment, the utopian is not concerned with abstract ideals that are independent of our lived bodily experience within the world. Instead, this thought, as it contemplates, for example, the good or the just situation, has its ground in our bodies. Thus, by placing the body in front of us, these experiences enable us to understand something previously hidden. Before we consider Merleau-Ponty more closely, I want to make some preliminary clarifications.

Our first concern is terminology. In this chapter I will use terminology that is both intentional and paradoxical. We should not fear the paradoxical for, as Kierkegaard reminds us, "the paradox is the passion of thought, and the thinker without a paradox is like the lover without passion: a mediocre fellow" (Kierkegaard, 1985: 37). This dictum should be kept in mind as we proceed. In this light, I will adopt the paradoxical prefix *pre* (as used with pre-schematically schematizes, pre-logical logic, and *pre*-primordial) to indicate the following. First, this prefix will be used to raise the issue of how the body "knows." That is, I will be assuming, not arguing that the body knows in a pre-noetic, pre-logical, pre-cognitive way.[5] Second, and important for my purposes, I will use this prefix to indicate something before the pre (of which we cannot speak). I have in mind specifically, borrowing from Emmanuel Levinas' linguistic strategy, the idea of ethics being prior to everything, albeit in a way that is not how this phrase "ethics-first" is used in most contemporary projects.[6] When he talks about the priority of ethics as a first philosophy it is not so much as that which substitutes for metaphysics in the canonic order of first philosophy. Rather, it is that which is so prior that in fact it is prior to the prioritization; so prior, we might say, that it is *prior to* the very order of philosophical discourse. So, it is a pre-philosophical priority at which the *pre* can only gesture. And to this end, whenever I use the *pre* in conjunction with, say, that which pre-schematically schematizes, I will have in mind this certain pre-logical priority. Third, and related, such indications are necessary for my purposes in order to be faithful in speaking and writing of the body (along with "flesh" in the following chapter). If the body knows in a pre-cognitive manner, then it is our philosophical obligation to think and write differently. It is extremely difficult, if not impossible, to speak in a demonstrative fashion about something like the body which does not know demonstratively in proofs or fixed ordering. What the body reveals is that it is not *episteme* as we have traditionally construed it because *episteme* is the project of demonstrative knowledge. In exploring the very idea of the bodily basis of utopian thought, then, our task is to speak and write differently and in a way that does not betray the body of which we attempt to speak and write. As a result of this problem, we are in need of markers that indicate this difficulty. But, and this we must not lose sight of, markers can *at best* only gesture to this difficulty and acknowledge the indeterminacy of such gesturing. My use of the prefix *pre* is such a gesture or qualification to alert the reader that I am aware of the complexity of this terminological predicament.

The second overall remark has to do with the language of *structure*. Rather than discussing how I will specifically use this term, I will explain it relative to the context in which it appears. The context to which I refer is not only a third clarification, but is perhaps the most important one in need of mentioning. I am speaking of the distinctions made in the following section between embodi*ment* and embodied*ness*. It is vital that we get clear on both the distinction and the relationship between the two because the focus of my argument in this chapter resides in the claim that our embodiment prefigures the utopian not only along the lines argued for in the previous chapter, but our embodiment as it relates to our lived bodily existence *is*, as we shall see with the case of Sojourner Truth below, the locus for the demand that things be better. Let me turn to embodiment.

When I speak of embodiment I mean certain structures *potentially* shared by all. Even though there are general features of embodiment which seem to be shared by humans, these structures, three of which I will return to later on, are not to be thought of as being fixed or timeless. As structures, they can be thought of in at least two ways because, as Merleau-Ponty himself notes, "Structure, like Janus, has two faces" (Merleau-Ponty, 1964b: 117). First, they can be thought of as structures that rigidly determine our embodiment/ embodied existence; structures that are necessary *and* sufficient; structures that establish determinate borders such as "inside" and "outside," "immanence" and "transcendence;" structures which, in effect, inscribe such demarcated lines rigorously; structures that *are* the meaning; and structures that, in this respect, might be regarded as transcendental. Or, second, these structures of embodiment could be thought of as those that open us up to the world in new and interesting ways; structures that are en-abling (as well as dis-abling); structures that empower us to break free from the narratives that have determinately defined us; structures that keep us moving within these ever present and not-wholly-transcendable determinations; structures that, because they are constantly in motion, are always in contention; and structures, in this respect, that might be appropriately labeled *quasi*-transcendental.[7]

Third, these structures of embodiment are not solely *in* us to be projected *out* onto the world. Likewise, the structures of embodiment are not *out* there in society waiting to be accessed. This is why whenever I speak of the utopian derived from the structures of embodiment I am not, as it were, speaking of *a* logic of embodiment but instead of logic*s* that are derived from an intertwining of embodiment within a particular horizon of bodily existence. To the extent that I speak or rather gesture towards an embodied utopian logic(s) I invoke a pre-primordial movement of utopian thought that is figured by our embodiment. But, to anticipate an objection, and as we will see more clearly in the next chapter with the discussion of "reversibility of flesh," this does not mean that we are destined for solipsism, individual nominalism or group essentialism. Rather, as I will argue in the following chapter, the notion of reversibility returns to us the universal element of the utopian, but a universal element that is of and from the particularity of lived bodily existence. So, how is embodiedness distinct from embodiment?

I will use embodied*ness* to designate the lived bodily experience of individuals as related to a particular socio-historical matrix. Therefore, I will use "embodiedness" and "lived bodily experience" interchangeably. On the one hand, we cannot speak of *one* inherent logic of the structures of embodiment, and, on the other hand, we can say that the logic(s) of the utopian thinking emerge out of embodiedness. Thus, the utopian is pre-schematically schematized by lived bodily experience, which means that "All interactions are opportunities for the progressive fleshing out of this originary schematism, this implicate order, this hint, in our intercorporeality, of a more *utopian* intercorporeality, concretely structured forms of reciprocity generated from within the shared body of social experience" (Levin, 1990: 43). Again, such a description is another way to convey my rejection of a rigid line of demarcation between the "in here" (immanence) and "out there" (transcendence) of embodiment. This does not mean the body does not "know" often what is "inside" and "outside." Precisely because lived bodily experience is about routine, bodily habits, and everyday bodily practices, lived bodily experience informs us as to what is acceptable and unacceptable, where boundaries exist, and how we are to act accordingly.

The structures of embodiment are forever colored and shaped by our embodiedness, or lived bodily experiences. Conversely, how we examine lived bodily experiences are shaped by, in this case, theoretical commitments to particular understandings of embodiment, which, as I have already stated, will be based on the work of Merleau-Ponty. Before we turn to the discussion that pursues the above distinctions more thoroughly, I would like to add one final note on terminology. In addition to using embodiment and embodiedness as described above, I will often use the more generic term "body" to denote *both* embodiment and embodiedness.

In the following section I examine three important structures of embodiment that highlight the bodily element of the utopian. In this section, unlike others, the components of my argument will emerge in conjunction with my reading of Merleau-Ponty's *Phenomenology of Perception*. I will not, however, remain simply at the level of reading this text, engaging in a type of philosophical journalism. Instead, my aim in what follows is to utilize Merleau-Ponty to develop a phenomenological understanding of the utopian. To accomplish this, I begin with the structure of transcendence.

The first structure of embodiment that is important for my discussion is the movement of transcendence. The notion of transcendence looms over the whole of Merleau-Ponty's work but is specifically introduced within his critique of empiricism and intellectualism as the paradox of transcendence and immanence.[8] In the *Phenomenology of Perception* Merleau-Ponty speaks of the paradox of transcendence and immanence as another way of thinking about the internal/external split, where the two are viewed as mutually exclusive— a problem that has plagued Western philosophy. Among other things, Merleau-Ponty, guided by his thesis of the primacy of perception, searches for a ground where immanence and transcendence intersect. The paradox of transcendence and immanence (and I would add, universal/particular, being/knowing, body schema/body image etc., and all of which Merleau-Ponty discusses) is a paradox for philosophical reflection that becomes less paradoxical whenever we involve ourselves with the things of the world. This, accordingly, is one task of philosophy: locate and explore those levels or forms of transcendence in human experience of the world. To this end, philosophy itself is an interactive process whereby the transcendent is allowed to disclose itself, and is why Merleau-Ponty can say:

> Reflection does not withdraw from the world towards the unity of consciousness as the world's basis; it steps back to watch the forms of transcendence fly up like sparks from a fire; it slackens the intentional threads which attach us to the world and thus brings them to our notice.... (PhP: xiii).

We can read this in the following way. We interact with things around us and realize that even though we can never fully separate ourselves from them, we are in some sense distinct from them. Thus, the transcendence intimated here as that which is grounded by and in our embodiment is a "symbiotic transcendence" (See Gill, 1991). It is not a reduction of the transcendent to the immanent; the movement of transcendence is retained. Second, it is an understanding of transcendence that highlights the movement or emergence from our common "intersubjectivity," or as Merleau-Ponty says elsewhere, our "intercorporeality" (see, for example, Merleau-Ponty, 1968). It is in and through this intercorporeality that we, as embodied beings, can transform and be transformed. Thus, to the degree that we speak of transcendence we do so with the understanding that it is always vigorously engaged within an environment. This is why Merleau-Ponty speaks of an "active transcendence," which is the "simultaneous contact with my own being and with the world's being" (PhP, 377). In this way, we can understand the notion of active transcendence along the lines of the way in which the body, as the locus of incarnation, houses, literally, the transcendence of the external demand that things will or can be different. In this regard, transcendence is the movement of action within a situated environment as the "act in which existence takes up, for its own purposes, and transforms such situation. Precisely because it is transcendence, existence never utterly outruns anything, for in that case the tension which is essential to it would disappear" (PhP, 169). Moreover, the in-breaking act of incarnation is the in-breaking of the universal into the particular, and, likewise, the particular as the site of the universal. It is an interruption. This dialectical move of the internal (incarnate body) and external (active transcendence) is one that signals the possibility of something new and better. In a word, the incarnate body is the site of revolution. This, at least, is how I read Merleau-Ponty when, in a very similar vein, he discusses the Incarnation of God. He writes:

> The Incarnation changes everything. Since the Incarnation, God has externalized. He was seen at a certain moment and in a certain place, and He left behind Him words and memories which were passed on. Henceforth, man's road toward God was no longer contemplation but the commentary and interpretation of that ambiguous message whose energy is never exhausted. In this sense, Christianity is diametrically opposed to "spiritualism." It reopens the question of the distinction between body and spirit, between interior and exterior (Merleau-Ponty, 1964b: 174-175).

Taken together, the emphasis on transcendence as action means that the openness of human existence is not that of an overarching telic principle that controls and determines everything (be it God, History, Reason, Nature, or Man), but instead a signaling of the intercorporeality of human beings as the site where, as a result, transcendence "no longer hangs over man: he becomes, strangely, its privileged bearer (Merleau-Ponty, 1964b: 71).[9]

Thus, active transcendence is not reduced to a fixed, static horizon against which we move and have our being. Neither is it reduced to the conceptual category of immanence. Instead, transcendence is a symbiotic relationship between the two and is about being-as-becoming *and* becoming-as-being. Accordingly, the utopian can be viewed as thought that is an impossibility for a future realization of something that is or can be *completely* settled and fixed. It is, to bring this discussion into the context of the previous chapter, the possibility of interruption carried out by the dialectical movement of active transcendence within the horizon of determinative incarnate relationships. In the end, the structure of (active) transcendence is that through which "the severity of the wrenching, twisting movement out of the surveillance and authority of our normalcy and identity" we can generate new understandings (Scott, 1997: 17).

To be sure, when I speak of embodiment as a movement of transcendence I am connecting this movement with the other two structures of embodiment I will discuss below, all of which are important to my argument in this chapter. For now, I want to emphasize that in speaking of embodiment *as* the order of transcendence I am aware that order can be a potential trap for the return of some fixed teleological notion of the utopian and despite my phenomenological orientation can be viewed as another pathological return of conventional utopian thought. I will return to this notion of order at the end of the chapter, but here I should add that as long as it is seen as a movement, any such ordering is itself a movement of withdrawal. To speak of an ordering in this light is to speak of an ordering that too withdraws, which means that, as a structure of embodiment as the movement of transcendence, it resists fixity, stasis, and resists becoming another normative ground by which we organize all other knowledge and action; embodiment as movement of transcendence resists being simply another "myth of the given" in two ways. On the one hand, embodiment as a structure that itself may be constituted as a foundation, is always-already compromised once the lived bodily conditions are considered. On the other hand, the dialectical relationship between our particular (lived existence), and the universal (structure of embodiment) means that *neither* the particular *nor* the universal is final, but instead the universal is the particular and this is always materially conditioned and never transparently accessed.

To speak of embodiment-as-the-movement-of-transcendence in this context, then, is to say that embodiment, first, is the *genesis* of utopian thinking because the body, like transcendence, withdraws itself from theory and resists totalizing efforts at theorizing it. We can speak of the bodily *basis* of the utopian but not as an *arche* for such thought where this means that embodiment/embodiedness serves as another first principle that guides all thought, utopian or otherwise. To do so would be to possess an understanding of transcendence not as movement but rather as fixed and determinate. Second, to speak of the body in this originary way is to invoke *genesis*, which owes much to the Greek understanding of *gignomai*, which is best translated as *happening, becoming*, what I would like to call *the encounter*. To propose that the body is the genesis of utopian thinking is to highlight an aspect that is inherent in the structure of embodiment, namely, a structure of embodiment that originates in a disruptive encounter. Seen as such, embodiment becomes the horizon of both beginning and end but most importantly the horizon of *disruption*, which opens up the potentiality of humans to transform themselves and their environments. In this regard, the body as the basis for utopian thought is a pre-primordial ground of open potentialities and is concerned with the *encounter* of the utopian rather than the fixed and determinate point of reference in the future, uncontaminated by any historical or bodily contingencies.

In sum, just as embodiment is a figure of transcendence, it is also that which marks and indicates one's position, an indication of thought, to be sure, but above all, of one's body first and foremost. The event of such thought does not take place outside of the circle of embodiment. Instead, the movement of utopian thinking as a bodily activity is a response to the horrific and impossible situations we find ourselves in from either our own choosing or external choices imposed on us. Thus, to be *u-topian* is not to have an anchored, theoretical position; that is, a theoretical position secured and fixed for all time. Instead it is a position, but a position grounded in embodiment because life moves; it does not stand still. To the degree, then, that we think the utopian anew we do so always grounded in this structure of embodiment-as-the-movement-of-transcendence. The result is that the utopian is not only the matter of projecting something that may or may not be (im)possible, but, like embodiment itself, it is the event.

We cannot think embodiment and lived bodily experience in isolation. The structures of embodiment are always understood via lived bodily experiences. Thus, understood in light of lived bodily experience the structure of transcendence, which illuminates the open potentialities of embodiment, can produce what Iris Young has called an *ambiguous* transcendence (see Young, 1990b: 147ff). Young defines this ambiguous transcendence in reference to both the calling-forth potential of the lived body and the potential restrictions to this capacity, which she designates as being overlaid with immanence.

> Now, once we take the locus of subjectivity and transcendence to be the lived body rather than pure consciousness, all transcendence is ambiguous because the body as natural and material is immanence. But it is not the ever-present possibility of any lived body to be passive, which I am referring to here as the ambiguity of the transcendence of the feminine lived body. . . . [In some instances] a woman typically refrains from throwing her whole body into a motion, and rather concentrates motion in one part of the body alone, while the rest of the body remains relatively immobile. Only part of the body, that is, moves outward toward a task, while the rest remains rooted in immanence (Young, 1990b: 148).

Young's description, while helpful in illustrating my point that the structures of embodiment (transcendence) are always intertwined with lived bodily experience, does not make the point as clearly as it could be made. In fact, I think her (over?) emphasis on the overlaying of *immanence* can invert the paradigm she wishes to problematize. By focusing, as she does throughout this discussion, on the immanence which limits the potential structure of transcendence, she tends to lose the thread of the movement of transcendence, something that is still important even for her own analysis of embodiment. It is important, and this point must be emphasized, because she, like I am claiming, suggests that we *all* potentially possess the structure of transcendence even if it is often impeded and thus becomes ambiguous.

Her central point worth retaining is that transcendence *is* a structure of embodiment. However, because this structure cannot be purely described or accessed it can either be a movement of potentialities or, because of certain social, economic, or physiological constraints that restrict, constrict and construct us (which is how I am interpreting her use of immanence), it can in fact regulate these potentials in such a way that they become confined, severely limited and hidden. Her example is throwing a ball. Such constriction takes place at the level of throwing a ball where a woman, because of certain restrictions, throws a ball with different bodily comportments. However, such restrictions can take place on other more metaphysical levels such as, for example, what it means to be "female," "male," or "black." In short, an ambiguous transcendence lets us know that, even though we may wish that the structure of transcendence be uncontaminated by our situatedness, it is not nor can it ever be thought or discussed as a pure eidetic structure. There are, consequently, two points worth emphasizing.

First, Young, whose work is infused by Merleau-Ponty's phenomenology and whose work seeks to bridge this with issues of gender difference, *still* suggests with her *ambiguous transcendence* the existence of a structure of embodiment similar to the one I have been arguing for: transcendence as movement and potential. Second, and where she extends and builds on Merleau-Ponty, she shows how such structures of embodiment (transcendence) are always understood relative to one's lived bodily experience and can thus be either a fulfillment of embodied potentialities or, as her analysis convincingly illustrates, a limit to such potentialities. What she illustrates for us is how precisely the structure of transcendence is *always* understood via lived bodily experience.

The second structure of embodiment significant to my purpose is that of intentionality. Intentionality is pre-primordial and manifests the movement of utopian thought in that, like transcendence, it possesses an unmediated openness to potential. In this regard, intentionality is not simply an intentionality of the act, which would be to remain within the horizon of Husserlian phenomenology. Instead, what is presupposed in the intentionality of the act is, according to Merleau-Ponty, an "operative intentionality," which is a broader understanding of intentionality in that it "produces the natural and antepredicative unity of the world and of our life, being apparent in our desires, our evaluations and in the landscape we see, more clearly than in objective knowledge ... ." (PhP, xviii). In this light, intentionality can be thought of as a part of the "active transcendence of consciousness," but also as an intentionality that encompasses all of experience whereby we have the potential to form new meanings in light of new intentions. As Merleau-Ponty states, "To understand is to experience the harmony between what we aim at and what is given, between the intention and the performance— and the body is our anchorage in a world" (PhP, 144). Anchorage here should not be read as an *arche*, which I described above. Rather, the body-as-intentionality here should be understood as that which *both* constitutes and is constituted by our world, another way of avoiding the distinction between "inside" and "outside" of embodiment. What is further acknowledged and opposed to the reading that intentionality is *our* construction of the world is that intentionality cannot be understood solely as an act of consciousness. Insofar as intentionality is a movement of embodiment, it is a kinesthetic intentionality that relies on bodily tactility within a particular environment; we are as much shaped by our situatedness as we shape it. In this relationship the order of priority is unknown and really unimportant. Rather, the important point is what Merleau-Ponty says in the following passage.

I *have* the world as an incomplete individual, through the agency of my body as the potentiality of this world, and I have the positing of objects through that of my body, or conversely the positing of my body through that of objects, not in any kind of logical implication, as we determine an unknown size through its objective relations to given sizes, but in a real implication, and because my body is a movement towards the world, and the world my body's point of support (PhP, 350).

The structure of intentionality is that of being-in-the-world, which is a way of saying that embodiment is ultimately "to be intervolved in a definite environment, *to identify oneself with certain projects continually committed to them*" (PhP, 82). The following remarks from Merleau-Ponty illustrate this point further. Such a statement is significant for my purposes because, in addition to the other passages from Merleau-Ponty, the ideas here reveal the notions I have not only already suggested are important to reconsidering the utopian, but ideas that I will return to later on in other chapters. Briefly, these are, first, the notion of fidelity or commitment to an event and, second the universal impetus of the utopian that, even though it originates in lived bodily experiences, is still a part of what he will later call "universal flesh." Merleau-Ponty alludes to some of these when he writes:

What makes me a proletarian is not the economic system or society considered as systems of impersonal forces, but these institutions as I *carry them within me and experience them*; nor is it an intellectual operation devoid of motive, by my way of being in the world within this institutional framework (PhP, 443, emphasis added).

This claim reveals how Merleau-Ponty himself is aware of this environment-body/body-environment relationship. Similarly, in a different text he writes the following.

But economic life is at the same time the historical carrier of mental structures, just as our body maintains the basic features of our behavior beneath our varying moods; and this is the reason one will more surely get to know the essence of a society by analyzing interpersonal relations as they have been fixed and generalized in economic life than through an analysis of the movements of fragile, fleeting ideas—just as one gets a better idea of man from his conduct than his thought (Merleau-Ponty, 1964a: 108).

Intentionality, then, is perhaps best described as the "I can" of the body. Intentionality as a pre-primordial act is our ability to orient ourselves within a given environment and act within that situation. It is expressed in the very ability to reach out and turn the handle to open the door. It is also expressed in my ability to become a philosopher or carpenter or a number of other potentialities given my situation. As a structure of embodiment, however, intentionality is limited; we cannot do just anything. No matter how much I want to fly I cannot fly like a bird because of the intentional constraints of embodiment. But there are, nevertheless, wide ranges of potentialities for me given my circumstances. Or, because of the impediments brought on by an accident or disease I may not be able to even move a cup across my desk. What is important to note here, as with transcendence, is that intentionality as a structure of embodiment communicates the *potential* for possibility inherent in our lives as much as the impossibility of certain things not being able to be actualized. Accordingly, the potentiality of utopian possibility is in tension, dialectically speaking, with the impossibility of (complete) actualization. In this way, then, intentionality, like that of transcendence, speaks of becoming and participates in the movement of thought, which can be either forward-looking or not. But, as we saw above, this movement of transcendence as a bodily movement of intentionality is not a movement without limits; it is a movement grounded in lived bodily experience. These forward-looking capabilities, to the extent that they remain forward-looking, are co-dependent on our "intercorporeality."

To keep the distinction being made throughout fresh in our minds, it is worth stating again that even though I refer to the structure of intentionality as an example of the movement of utopian thought grounded in the body, I am not saying that this bodily intentionality, or these forward-looking possibilities, are "in" the body to be acted "on" the outside world. Such a claim would be to retain the subject/object split Merleau-Ponty problematized. Instead, bodily intentionality, while being referred to as a structure of embodiment is *always* understood relative to one's lived bodily experience. Before examining this more closely we need to say one more thing about intentionality.

Intentionality must be understood within the context of bodily motility. Motility can be understood within the following parameters. First, there exists in embodiment a tension between a "thereness" and "hereness." "There" has the potential to become a "here." Merleau-Ponty speaks of this in terms of bodily space, which can be transformed into objective space. The body is active in this process in its ability to experience intentionality through its motility.

> By considering the body in movement, we can see better how it inhabits space (and, moreover, time) because movement is not limited to submitting passively to space and time, it actively assumes them, it takes them up in their basic significance which is obscured in the commonplaces of established situations (PhP, 102).

Bodily motility, then, includes our physical capacities, our bodily limitations, and our body's ability to pursue and consequently fulfill goals. An example of this is the shape or color of one's body. Ideally, one has the potential to become lots of things one chooses. However, because so many people experience their world as "epidermalized" their potentialities are thwarted by virtue of how dominant discourses define them. What is more, such an epidermalizing of one's world does not take place exclusively at the institutional level of government, education, or other institutions responsible for dominant discourses. Instead, certain people are defined as different, unable to "be" certain things, and are consequently "other" because their bodies and identities are marked by mundane levels of looks, speech, movement and/or other gestures that define them as "this" or "that."[10]

A concrete example of this is someone like Barack Obama. Joe Biden, now Obama's Vice-President, caused a stir when, in the early stages of Obama's candidacy Biden said "I mean, you got the first mainstream African-American who is articulate and bright and clean and a nice-looking guy...I mean, that's a storybook, man" (*USA TODAY*, 2007). Many interpreted this as a version of "he does not talk or sound like a black man." Now, whether Biden meant this is not my concern. Rather, my point is that this is a instance of the process of epidermalizing. In the case of Obama, this involves the following. First, black people (black bodies) are marked by certain intonations, inflections etc. Second, Obama is thought by many to be "O.K." because he does not talk like a black man, the implication being that he speaks more like us (usually read white). More to the point here is the question of Obama's "blackness." Would Obama still have been elected had he spoke in a thick, ghetto accent? One could easily argue no, and in doing so make the point that this black man's hopes of living out his potentialities would probably never come to fruition because, among other things, his black body marked by society in certain ways would prevent this. The point: such markings impede potentialities.

Like other structures of embodiment, motility is pre-reflective and it is that wisdom of the body which enables us to orient ourselves to a particular given situation, summon that which can make sense of this present, and empower us to alter the situation if needed. But what happens if this capacity is lost? Put in terms of my argument here, bodily motility, as the body's synthetic and projective capability of pre-schematically schematizing how we think about the movement of the utopian, is important for this utopian structure of embodiment for the following reasons. First, motility enables pre-thematized possibilities to become thematized, expressed, and acted upon. Second, motility provides the foundation for spatial orientation whereupon multiple imaginative projections are seen. Third, motility supplies a framework for abstract movement. At its basic level motility possesses the power of giving meaning, in which "the meaning of all significance is engendered in the domain of represented space" (PhP, 142). The acquisition of habit is an example. Through the incorporation of certain habits into the "bulk of our own body" (PhP, 143), we are able to mark ourselves in the world, discover a number of different aims or gestures, all of which render understanding possible. This is why "To understand is to experience the harmony between what we aim at and what is given, between the intention and the performance—and the body is our anchorage in the world" (PhP, 144). It is the body's ability to bring harmony out of such distinct notions that pre-schematically schematizes utopian thinking. Our bodily projection through motility, working in concert, enables us to, "mark out boundaries and directions in the given world, to establish lines of force, to keep perspectives in view, in a word, to organize the given world in accordance with the projects of the present moment, to build into the geographical setting a behavioral one, a system of meanings outwardly expressive of the subjects internal activity" (PhP, 112).

If this bodily motility is diminished or incapacitated, then our ability to organize the present through a summoning of the past is thwarted as is our ability to alter our situation. Accordingly, if the utopian is grounded in bodily motility and intentionality, and if these are somehow diminished, then our ability to keep open the movement of the utopian is likewise reduced. But notice here: reduced *not* eradicated. The point in saying this is that these structures inform bodily movement at a level so fundamental that if they are in fact diminished, we have trouble seeing the hidden potentials whether in mundane actions such as moving a glass or more important possibilities such as becoming President. We find this idea suggested by Merleau-Ponty when he describes this loss as a difference between "normal" and "morbid" motility.

> The normal person *reckons with* the possible, which thus, without shifting from its position as a possibility, acquires a sort of actuality. In the patient's case [whose motility is morbid], however, the field of actuality is limited to what is met with in the shape of a real contact or is related to these data by some explicit process of deduction (PhP, 109).

Merleau-Ponty's language here might be problematic because "morbid" connotes abnormal. However, these morbid elements of intentionality suggest helpfully that abnormality signals what really happens when intentionality is lost. Let's consider another example of such a loss.

People with normal motility can project imaginary situations, assess them and act to bring them about. They can experience their body as that which mediates the world, enables them to inhabit such space, and that which, in its constant movement, adjusts to situations as needed so that certain bodily potentials can be revealed. With normal motility they do not "mistake imaginary situations for reality, but extricate their real bodies from the living situation to make them breathe, speak, and if need be, weep in the realm of imagination" (PhP, 105). In other words, normal motility enables one to fully come to grips with their body as a medium aware of its kinesthetic presence that opens new potentialities. When this motility is adversely effected this projective power is lost. One who no longer has the capability of bringing about projections experiences his or her body as "congealed, whereas for the normal person his projects polarize the world, bringing magically to view a host of signs which guide action, as notices in a museum guide visitors" (PhP, 112).

This example helps us to see more clearly something briefly mentioned earlier, namely, that the body's motility through intentionality empowers us to use our bodies as "a means to play acting." This inability of "play-acting" is directly linked to one's ability to "place oneself for a moment in an imaginary situation, to find satisfaction in changing one's 'setting'" (PhP, 135). *This ability is, no less, the originary pre-logical logic of the utopian pre-schematically schematized by the movement of embodiment, which, when diminished or lost, adversely affects our ability to keep alive the movement of transcendence and subsequently causes us to cover over hidden utopian potential.* In other words, when the structure of intentionality through motility is lost or diminished, it is extremely difficult to move beyond our present situation, summon the past, and project a (presumably) better future. Merleau-Ponty explains this loss in the following passage and, I would add, intimates its effect on our ability to think the movement of the utopian.

> The patient [whose capacities for projections have been diminished] cannot enter into a fictitious situation without converting it into a real one: he cannot tell the difference between a riddle and a problem. . . . Future and past are for him only "shrunken" extensions of the present. . . . [H]e is "tied" to actuality, he "lacks liberty," that concrete liberty which comprises the general power of putting oneself into a situation (PhP, 135).

Motility illuminates the event of the utopian insofar as it enables us to embody "a more fundamental function, a vector mobile in all directions like a searchlight, one through which we can direct ourselves toward anything, in or outside ourselves, and display a form of behaviour in relation to that object" (PhP, 136). But, as Merleau-Ponty quickly points out, it is more than this because this searchlight analogy presupposes a given object at which we aim (another instance of avoiding the strict "in"/ "out" demarcation of embodiment/world). To augment this image, we need the additional idea of *intentional arc*. If bodily motility is diminished to the point of disallowing organization and projection, then we cannot conceptualize an alternative scenario because our bodies will not allow it. This is because, as I said earlier, our bodily motility is at its most basic level the "I can" of our lived bodily experience. Bodily motility draws on and is influenced by our intentional arc, which summarizes pointedly the gesture of utopian capabilities exemplified by our lived bodily experience. This intentional arc "projects round about us our past, our future, our human setting, our physical, ideological and moral situation, or rather which results in our being situated in all these respects. It is this intentional arc which brings about the unity of the senses, of sensibility and motility. And it is that which goes limp in illness" (PhP, 136). This, I suggest, is a way to understand the utopian at its best and, simultaneously, the utopian as it becomes pathological.

In the end, this intentional arc is the body's ability to sense its own movements and gestures; a sensing that draws together its past experiences into and through the present ones, and anticipating an alternative final position. But as we saw with the structure of transcendence, and as we saw with certain markings of people deemed other, all is not clear once lived bodily experience is factored. What happens to the structures of intentionality and motility seen in reference to lived bodily experience? Again let us return to Young.

Just as with transcendence Young says that intentionality in motility can, because of social circumstance, be hidden. She refers to this as *inhibited intentionality*. We can understand this notion by locating it relative to the "I can" of intentionality and motility. The intentionality of embodiment, to be sure, possesses an "I can," but often we do not, either by our own choosing or situational circumstances, enable these potentialities. In this regard, lived bodily experience dictates to us an "I cannot," which can be either internal or external (Young, 1990b: 148). Again, our example earlier of Barack Obama and a black man from the inner city whose accent is distinctly black reiterates this point. While we might be tempted to think that the body exudes an uninhibited intentionality insofar as the body can project and aim, organize and unify itself in light of this aim, the body can find that, because of an injury or societal markings, its ability to project an aim is constrained in one way or another.

Addressing female bodily experience, Young describes how an inhibitedness thwarts intentionality in the following way.

> Feminine motion often severs this mutually conditioning relation between aim and enactment [in Merleau-Ponty]. In those motions that when properly performed require the coordination and directedness of the whole body upon some definite end, women frequently move in contradictory a way. Their bodies project an aim to be enacted but at the same time stiffen against their performance of the task. In performing a physical task the woman's body does carry her toward the intended aim, often not easily and directly, but rather circuitously, with the wasted motion resulting from the effort of testing and reorientation, which is a frequent consequence of feminine hesitancy.

> For any lived body, the world appears as the system of
> possibilities that are correlative to its intentions. For any lived
> body, moreover, the world also appears to be populated with
> opacities and resistances correlative to its own limits and
> frustrations. For any bodily existence, that is, an "I cannot" may
> appear to set limits to the "I can" (Young, 1990b: 149).

Here again Young does not deny the existence of certain structures
like intentionality and motility. Rather, I take her point in pursuing such
an investigation of female bodily comportment to be that the structures
of intentionality and motility do not themselves exist in pure eidetic
form, but emerge within lived bodily experience. With transcendence,
intentionality and motility in place, we can now understand more clearly
the parallel between the order of embodiment and the utopian.

One of the things that we can say in light of the above discussion
is that there is a synthetic capability of embodiment. I want to refer
to this as the utopian order of embodiment. We must be cautious in
using such a term because in speaking of the order of embodiment we
must be careful not to suggest something that betrays embodiment as
movement. When I speak of an order of embodiment I have in mind
the following. It is meant to convey an ordering that exists *before* any
kind of schematization occurs; an order that is neither completely
determined nor determinate but an order, nevertheless, that attunes
us to the pre-ordered embodied intentionality-as-potentialities. This is
why I would want, by way of a gesture, to speak of this order as an order
that pre-schematically schematizes the motivations of embodiment.
Such a notion of the order of embodiment is important for how we not
only think but speak about the bodily basis for utopian thought. As an
order grounded in the movement of transcendence, intentionality and
motility, this language of ordering speaks directly to the constructive
or re-constructive nature of embodiment, both of which are raised by
any discussion of utopian thought. Such discussions ultimately bring
us back to the bodily basis of such thought. What is the order in this
bodily basis? Does the body *con*struct? *Re*-construct? How does such an
ordering elicit the event of utopian thought?

In the light of what I have been arguing, I would say that as an order of active transcendence, intentionality and motility, the body is potentially constructive in the sense that via the body openness to the utopian potential is possible. While not completely chaotic, embodiment as the movement of transcendence is such that it remains floating, as it were, and that which does not close in upon itself like moves to reconstruction are so apt to make. The order of embodiment is again better thought of as consisting in a pre-logical order that is "in need of further socialization. Society's work of socialization, and its vision of moral development, should respect, and be responsive to, the primal order of sociality already inherent in the...body" (Levin, 1990: 37).

Let me say by way of summary that as the ordering of embodiment we project onto an environment purposes, intentions, and aims that we are not always able to unify and synthesize. This is so because even though we project onto an environment we are not, as we have seen, the sole constituting agents of those environments. Such a claim would be to lapse back into a form of immanentalism Merleau-Ponty seeks to overcome. The order, to the degree that there is one, enables us to know something of our narrative make-up, assess it, and transform it if necessary. However, and just as important, this order of embodiment, because it is linked with the movement of transcendence and intentionality, reveals an "ambiguous mode of existing" (PhP, 198). Thus, the order, to the degree that it is ordered, is always moving, never fixed; always open, never closing off the possibility of something new. It is an order of thought that, as movement and event, unsettles our assurances of the same.

This order of embodiment is not always one of unity. As we have seen, when we look at lived bodily experience the apparent unity is really one of *discontinuous unity* (Young, 1990b: 149). In keeping with the language of order we could just as easily say that the structure of order understood in light of lived bodily experience can be one of non-order. That is, it is an ordering not directed at anything, a non-ordering that lacks any bodily unity at all. As such the dis-continuity or non-ordering interrupts the ordering in new ways. I would add, however, that such non-ordering is still within the horizon of becoming, within the movement of transcendence, because, as non-ordering, it ruptures a determinate ordering and produces thought that is itself anticipatory. But this non-ordering still nevertheless occurs with the determinate horizon of ordering and as such, even in its non-ordering, keeps the movement of utopian thought open.

Embodiedness ruptures the received views of constructed categories such as race and gender, which are, to be sure, more fluid but powerful nevertheless in the ways they constitute our self-identities. Another good illustration of this is the life of Sojourner Truth. Consider the following portion of her famous "Ain't I a Woman" speech.

> That man over there says women need to be helped into carriages, and lifted over ditches, and to have the best place everywhere. Nobody ever helps me into carriages, or over mud-puddles, or gives me any best place! And ain't I a woman? Look at me! Look at my arm! I have ploughed, and planted, and gathered into barns, and no man could head me! And ain't I a woman? I could work as much and eat as much as a man—when I could get it— and bear the lash as well! And ain't I a woman? I have borne thirteen children, and seen most of them sold off to slavery, and when I cried out with my mother's grief, none but Jesus heard me! And ain't I a woman? (As quoted in Collins, 1990: 14).

This powerful speech suggests the following. First, the constitutive narrative identity of an African-American and a woman in nineteenth-century America is essentially one where both are deemed unworthy of the title "human." One result of this narrative framework is the dehumanization and degradation of many African-Americans and women. In opposition, Truth's own embodied experience, as Patricia Hill Collins remarks, shatters this narrative identity by "exposing a concept as ideological or culturally constructed rather than as natural or a simple reflection of reality" (Collins, 1990: 14). In its place, Truth's bodily interaction within this oppressive narrative suggests something different about what it means to be black, feminine and a woman. Yet instead of this alternative being based on disembodied and disembedded principles common to every "rational" person, Truth's vision for a society, rid of the degradation and dehumanization of people of color and women, relies on mundane bodily activities such as eating, child-birthing, ploughing, and planting. As such, her bodily experiences accomplish something that normative political philosophies of her time are unable to do, which is to take seriously bodily phenomena as the locus for engaging oppression and constructing alternative pictures of reality. What this example reveals is the following. First, the utopian moment is grounded in the body. That is, as a figure of the utopian, lived bodily experience keeps open the ability to reflect differently on the topics of society, empowers us to explore alternate visions, and, most importantly, moves us to risk our (embodied) selves to keep open this movement of the utopian. Second, and related, our bodily experiences can either reinscribe oppressive narratives or radically call them into question.

What I have tried to offer in this chapter is a way to think of the utopian as a bodily activity. Through an analysis of Merleau-Pontian structures of embodiment we have seen how the body carries with it the utopian schematic whereby we encounter our world in an oppressive or dehumanizing way and, as a result, understand it or transform it in and through those lived bodily experiences that often begin in *pathos* that is disruptive. To fashion such an alternative we do not rely on dis-embodied principles of the just, the good, or the right, but, instead, derive our action from the particulars of lived bodily experience that, in the case of Sojourner Truth, represent the universal call of the utopian demand that things be better, an element that calls for responsibility as I will argue in Chapter Five.

We have seen that inherent in the lived body is a structure of potentiality, which correlates to bodily intentions. First, the body projects an aim at which it directs itself. Second, the body gathers and synthesizes itself with its surroundings, albeit a synthesis that is always in tension with its surroundings. Third, through its relationship with itself and its projected alternatives the lived body gets its shape and potentially re-shapes its surroundings toward something new. Fourth, this ability to gather is primordial and is the act by which we not only gather ourselves toward projected aims, but an act by which we are gathered with others. As Merleau-Ponty notes, we "do not bring together one by one the parts of my body" this translation and this unification are performed once and for all within me; they are my body itself" (PhP, 150). I have demonstrated that the utopian is grounded in the truth of our body, its natural movements, and its interrelatedness with others. This bodily felt sense of utopian awareness, we might say, is a more organic notion that views the body as that vehicle that reveals to us the universal call of justice, right, or good, all of which are at the heart of the utopian. A question, however, begins to emerge in the context of my focus on embodiment, embodiedness and the lived bodily experience of individuals. This is: "How, with the focus on the (individual) body does the utopian manage the universal call (the best of the utopian impulse) for collective action?" In other words, if we focus solely too much on the "bodily element of the utopian," where this is a focus on the individual, do we not undermine the universal dimension inherent in the utopian at its best? The answer, I submit, is no. Just as in this chapter, the work of Merleau-Ponty, especially his later work, can help us to think about this question, in particular his understanding of the "reversibility of universal flesh." This will be the focus of the following chapter.

Chapter Four

Forever Together: Reversibility and the Politics of Utopian Possibility

In her provocative yet highly controversial book *Eichmann in Jerusalem,* Hannah Arendt suggests that Eichmann's participation in the Nazi extermination of six million Jews was due in large part to his "inability to think from the standpoint of somebody else" (Arendt, 1963: 49). In short, Eichmann was unable to reverse perspectives with those whose death that he commissioned. Had he been able to do this, Arendt implies, Eichmann could have recognized the suffering he caused and thus would have either ceased it or taken measures to halt these senseless acts. Arendt's implication here is that the ability to *reverse perspectives* is essential to moral reasoning and transformative politics. She would be as controversial today as she was in 1963 for holding this position.

Arendt would no doubt still be criticized for her "banality of evil" thesis, but, also for her insistence on the reversibility of perspectives. This position, as the argument goes, assumes a transparency between subjects and consequently does violence to the other. That which Arendt suggests is an idea central to moral reasoning and transformative politics, namely, the ability to think from another's perspective, would today be dismissed as ethically wrongheaded and politically devastating. Against those who want to reject something like reversibility as unwise, I argue for a notion of reversibility, based on an engagement with the later work of Merleau-Ponty as another key element in reconfiguring the utopian. There are three reasons why reversibility is important for my purposes.

First, reversibility, as we will see below, expresses a *universal* dimension to the utopian, which is a demand that once followed establishes a community of utopians. Second, reversibility addresses the question posed in the last chapter, namely, "If the utopian is embodied, and you have different bodies, then how do we avoid having as many understandings of the utopian as we have the bodies that encounter it?" It will be my claim that a phenomenological notion of reversibility is a resource for avoiding this implication and allows us to retain the universal impetus inherent in the demand of the utopian. Put more technically, reversibility signals a way to avoid two potential objections for retrieving the utopian. On the one hand, we want to avoid an understanding of the utopian that eradicates particularities under the guise of uniform autonomy. On the other hand, what we want to prevent in making the move to situatedness (embodied or otherwise) is either group essentialism or individual nominalism. The former is repeating the utopian in a way that makes the utopian not only conventional, but, as I argued earlier, irrelevant. The latter, which is the inverse of the former, is a way of repeating the utopian in the guise of the "politics of difference," and, despite what proponents of this orientation claim, deprives such movements of the universal impetus at the heart of any movement of justice, freedom and so forth. Finally, reversibility in a significant manner marks for us the way we are simultaneously held together, yet forever held apart. As such, reversibility signals the *gap* between finally coming together completely and remaining apart entirely. In this light, reversibility as the gap that constitutes both coming-together and remaining-apart interrupts our dreams of either complete shared understanding or utter isolation, and as such becomes itself an important element for reconsidering the utopian.

This point I am making is made in a similar way by Cornel West who, even though he does not invoke the idea of reversibility explicitly, nevertheless indicates the same sentiment when in his book *Race Matters* he claims that the 1992 Los Angeles riots taught us the lesson that "we are not connected in ways that we would like to be but also, in a more profound sense, . . . this failure to connect binds us even more tightly together." To avoid further fragmentation between people of differences he ends his introduction by telling us, "Either we learn a new language of empathy and compassion, or the fire this time will consume us all" (West, 1994: 18; 13). While we can agree with his sentiment, reversibility as I will develop below is not simply empathy and compassion by another name; in fact, I will, toward the end of this chapter, argue that reversibility is *not* an ethical notion at all. I am, however, getting ahead of myself. Before we can see this more clearly, it will first help us to understand both the historical interest in reversibility and how this notion has returned to contemporary political thinking.

If the contemporary interest in the reversibility of perspectives has its roots in the political philosophy of Hannah Arendt where she reclaims the Kantian notion of "enlarged mentality" then as we will see more clearly in the following section, it is Seyla Benhabib, more than any other contemporary political philosopher, who carries on this Arendtian notion and develops it relative to her own program of communicative ethics.[1] Additionally, Iris Young, herself indebted to Arendt, has criticized Benhabib on this point and proposed an alternative. The result of this dialogue is a profitable discussion of the importance of reversibility for political interaction, and an issue about which a Merleau-Pontian approach has something to say. I will argue that this Merleau-Pontian notion best fits with a non-conventional understanding of the utopian. Toward this end, I first want to summarize Arendt's position, second, recount the parameters of the Benhabib and Young discussion, and, finally, fashion a response to this debate from Merleau-Ponty that I extend to the discussion of the utopian. Let me begin with Arendt.

For Arendt enlarged thinking is the ability to think representatively. Her gloss on Kant's remark is summarized in two important places. The first, which appears in her *Lectures on Kant's Political Philosophy*, is more general in scope.

> [A]n "enlarged mentality" is the condition *sine qua non* of right judgment; one's community sense makes it possible to enlarge one's mentality. Negatively speaking, this means that one is able to abstract from private conditions and circumstances, which, as far as judgment is concerned, limit and inhibit its exercise.... Communicability obviously depends on the enlarged mentality;

one can communicate only if one is able to think from the other person's standpoint; otherwise one will never meet him, never speak in such a way that he understands. By communicating one's feelings, one's pleasures and disinterested delights, one tells one's *choices* and one chooses one's company. . . . (Arendt, 1982: 73-74).

The second passage provides a more thorough account of what enlarged thinking means in reference to the faculty of judgment.

The power of judgment rests on a potential agreement with others, and the thinking process which is active in judging something is not, like the thought process of pure reasoning, a dialogue between me and myself, but finds itself always and primarily, even if I am quite alone in making up my mind, in an anticipated communication with others with whom I must finally come to some agreement. From this potential agreement judgment derives its specific validity. This means, on the one hand, that such judgment must liberate itself from the 'subjective private conditions,' that is, from the idiosyncrasies which naturally determine the outlook of each individual in his privacy and are legitimate as long as they are only privately held opinions but which are not fit to enter the market place, and lack all validity in the public realm. And this enlarged way of thinking, which as judgment knows how to transcend its individual limitations, cannot function in strict isolation or solitude; it needs the presence of others 'in whose place' it must think, whose perspective it must take into consideration, and without whom it never has the opportunity to operate at all (Arendt, 1961: 220-221).

These passages contain much that would require detailed interpretation. However, for my purposes I will highlight four important points. First, enlarged thinking suggests that our opinions and ideas are affected by those with whom we interact. Our judgments and thinking have an indispensable communicative dimension that precludes us from making judgments in an isolated fashion. An enlarged mentality is not simply a private activity but a public matter in that one's private interests always affect others. Second, while enlarged thinking does mean thinking from the standpoint of the other it does not mean that we lose our identity or co-opt the identity of an other under our own. Enlarged thought here is to be understood within the framework of what might be called the movement of transcendence-as-alterity, which is to say we *attempt* to understand the position of the other in undistorted ways. Third, because we are always affected by others in our judgments, and these others remain other by virtue of their transcendence to us, certain spaces must be created where the perspectives of others can be articulated, yet contested, and transformed in order to insure a non-coercive and co-optive politics of enlarged mentality. Fourth, enlarged thinking is a quintessential *political* activity because it is a mode of thinking that empowers us to deal with the other in his or her particularity and still enables us to make claims to communal validity. This is why, for Arendt enlarged thinking is "the mode of thinking that is essential for politics—the debate, opinion formation, persuasion, and augmentation that are characteristic of action" (Bernstein, 1983: 217-218).[2] With this brief background in place, let me now discuss the resurgence of this concept.

Seyla Benhabib has proposed a reconsideration of this Arendtian concept and consequently propelled the notion of enlarged thinking back into contemporary political discussions.[3] Her work has been primarily fashioning a proposal of communicative ethics, with the notion of enlarged thinking, reciprocity and reversibility central to this project. The appropriation and modification of this Arendtian notion first received its most forceful treatment in Benhabib's essay on the generalized and the concrete other. The generalized and concrete other can be viewed either as mutually exclusive since they emphasize different views of the self, or on a continuum because "to think of universalizability as a reversing of perspectives and a seeking to understand the standpoint of the other(s), they must be viewed not only as generalized but also as concrete others" (Benhabib, 1992: 9-10)· There are two important steps in her argument.

First, the notion of the "generalized other" distinguishes individuals as rational beings who are entitled to the rights and privileges we would afford ourselves. This view of the self is such that "our relation to the other is governed by the norms of *formal equality and reciprocity*: each is entitled to expect and to assume from us what we can expect and assume from him or her" (Benhabib, 1992: 159). The notion of the generalized other allows me to claim the right (often viewed as a basic human right) to do or enjoy something and not expect hindrance from another in attempting to enjoy or do that which I see as a basic right. Even though the other is one who possesses particular characteristics, desires, wants and needs as an individual, what is emphasized as the defining trait of the other's moral dignity are not these individual wants, needs and desires but that which is held in common, namely, that the other like us is an acting and speaking rational agent. This means (1) each individual argues for his or her basic human rights; (2) there exists some "common human experience" against which individual experience could be judged and; (3) persons participating in this process reason and think similarly.

Second, the view of the self as "concrete other," however, highlights the fact that individuals are rational beings *with* various histories that shape their identity. This view suggests that we are governed by the norms of *equity*, and *complementary reciprocity*: each is entitled to expect and to assume from the other forms of behavior through which the other feels recognized and confirmed as a concrete, individual being with specific needs, talents and capacities. Our differences in this case complement rather than exclude one another. The focus here is on individuality where we attempt to comprehend the needs of the other along with the motivation (desires) that guides us in deliberations. Benhabib continues:

> These norms require in various ways that I exhibit more than the simple assertion of my rights and duties in the face of your needs. In treating you in accordance with the norms of friendship, love, and care, I confirm not only your *humanity* but your human *individuality*. The moral categories that accompany such interactions are those of responsibility, bonding and sharing. The corresponding moral feelings are those of love, care and sympathy and solidarity (Benhabib, 1992: 159).

Every person as a concrete other brings with them particular histories that have shaped their identity. Employing *complementary reciprocity* we would want to insure that every person receives forms of behavior that do not dismiss the otherness of his or her unique experience with specific needs, talents and capacities. In dealing with resolution of atrocities perpetrated on individuals, for instance, we would not disregard the generalized other which would be concerned with supplying "moral ideal of impartiality" that would "govern not only our *deliberations* in public but also the *articulation* of reasons by public institutions" (Ibid).

There are, then, two concluding points that this discussion of the generalized and concrete other reveals. First, we can not assume all people reason in the same fashion. The view of the self that follows from an exclusively generalized understanding and is both inattentive to the concrete selves that participate in the reasoning process and incapable of individuating among selves. Second, to the extent that we can speak of solidarity we do so in a way that does not completely fuse differing parties. Rather, each party is taken on her or his own terms as capable of seeing something different. From each location we are able, through dialogue, to generate connections that yield new possibilities for knowledge. The goal is to become exposed to and inclusive of those positions of which we both are and are not aware.

In this light, however, a question emerges: "How does Benhabib's proposal relate to the event of the utopian so that we can argue for norms that function in such a way as to enable us to bring critique, yet do so in a way that does not at best become irrelevant or at worst perpetuate a similar exclusivity or oppressiveness?" Here, I suggest, is where we benefit from Benhabib's addition to the Arendtian notion of enlarged thought. We are not only more proficient at practicing complementary reciprocity discussed earlier, but able to judge other claims and still remain open to modifying our own positions by possessing an enlarged mentality. Whereas Arendt describes enlarged thinking strictly in political terms, Benhabib expands it to encompass both our political and moral capabilities. Enlarged thinking seeks to bring as many perspectives to bear on one's own position without subsuming other positions into our own because, as she writes most recently, it is "a capacity for presenting to oneself the perspectivality of the world, of taking cognizance of the many points of view through which a matter must be seen and evaluated. This capacity is not empathy, in that it does not mean to "feel with others," but signifies instead a cognitive ability to "think with others"" (Benhabib, 1996a: 191). We can understand this notion more clearly by considering how Benhabib's argument, which like Arendt's before her, responds to original mention of this notion in Kant.

According to Benhabib, enlarged thought is distinct from either a formalistic understanding of the Kantian categorical imperative, on the one hand, or simply cultivating empathy, on the other hand. Based on a procedure of enlarged thought, the Kantian universal formula, "Act only according to that maxim whereby you can at the same time will that it should become a universal law," becomes, "Act in such a way that the maxim of your actions takes into account the perspective of everyone else in such a way that you would be in a position to "woo their consent"" (Benhabib, 1992: 136). In her response to Kant's universal formula of the Categorical Imperative as being able to "woo the consent" of others, Benhabib provides the following reformulation.

> For Kant this [distinguishing empathy from enlarged thinking] was not an issue since he assumed that, thinking for one, a pure rational being could think for all. If we reject Kantian a priorism, and his assumption that as moral selves we are all somehow identical; if, in other words, we distinguish a universalist morality of principles from Kant's doctrine of a priori rationality, then I want to suggest we must think of such enlarged thought as a condition of actual or simulated dialogue. To "think from the perspective of everyone else" is to know "how to listen" to what the other is saying, or when the voices of others are absent, to imagine to oneself a conversation with the other as my dialogue partner (Benhabib, 1992: 137).

The point worth emphasizing here is that the universalistic emphasis drawn from Kant is not dismissed but instead modified so that it is dependent on the multiple contexts out of which moral judgments are made. To think from the standpoint of everyone else requires the application of contextual moral and political judgment. To be sure, we do not cease in trying to convince the other of the merits of our own position. After all, we try to "woo the consent" of the other, which is another way of saying that the utopian besides being a disruptive moment figured by the body possesses a universal intent that demands a witness. As I will argue in the next chapter, whenever we posit our visions of a better world, after undergoing an interruptive event that we seek to make sense of, we *intend* our visions to be accepted by others. This is why we can never completely determine utopian thinking in such a way that insures total unanimity. Rather, the best we can hope for is to witness to the movement of such thought, among other things, through giving testimony to the other in his or her particularity, a particularity, as in the case of Sojourner Truth, that reveals the universal demand for justice itself.

Another important addition for understanding Benhabib's views on enlarged thinking is general interest, which functions to temper the potential pathology of the utopian. By pursuing a general interest we do not, contra John Rawls, necessarily aspire to complete "overlapping consensus" or unanimity.[4] Instead, general interest is that which allows us to argue from our situation for ideas to which all *could* consent, not must consent. Benhabib explains:

> I propose to view the concept of "general interest" in ethics and politics more as a regulative ideal and less as the subject matter of substantive consensus. In ethics, the universalizability procedure, if it is understood as a reversing of perspectives and the willingness to reason from the other's (others') point of view, does not guarantee consent; it demonstrates the will and the readiness to seek understanding with the other and to reach some reasonable agreement in an open-ended moral conversation. Likewise, in politics, it is less significant that "we" discover "the" general interest, but more significant that collective decisions be reached through procedures which are radically fair and open to all (Benhabib, 1992: 9).

The important distinction here is between "consensus" and "reaching an agreement." It is arguably the one point, as we will see shortly, on which Benhabib is most often misunderstood.

Benhabib rejects a notion of general interest that has as its goal the un-covering and dis-covering of rational criteria available to all. Moreover, the goal is not one in which fundamental particularities, often the locus of much disagreement, are constrained whether beforehand or in the dialogical process in order for consensus to be procured.[5] Such a conception of general interest would be a by-product of viewing the other solely as a generalized other. Rather, the concept of general interest opposes fixed and context-independent principles of universalizability. Furthermore, to speak of general interest does not mean that we treat dissenting voices as mere anomalies to the larger more dominant theories. General interest, linked with the practice of enlarged thinking, means that we can be aware of and entertain the multiplicity of *all* voices including the disenfranchised, and that these voices do not have to agree upon a number of premises *before* genuine dialogue takes place. As Benhabib writes:

> Above all these decisions should not exclude the voice of those whose "interests" may not be formulable in the accepted language of public discourse, but whose very presence in public life may force the boundaries between private needs and public claims, individual misfortunes and collectively representable grievances (Benhabib, 1992: 9).

In the end, general interest and enlarged thought function together so that we can at once remain sensitive to differences and still engage in social critique with the hope of "wooing" those whose vision for the world differs from ours.

Benhabib's interest in enlarged thinking has not gone without questioning. Iris Young, whose work we encountered in the previous chapter, more than any other political philosopher has criticized Benhabib on several points mentioned above. Young's critique against Benhabib runs as follows. First, the language of reciprocity and mutuality, central to Benhabib, is a longing for harmony where consensus and complete mutuality rule the day. Second, and what I think is the most serious of Young's criticisms, Benhabib embodies what Young, following Derrida, calls the idea of the "copresence of subjects" where various subjects become transparently represented to one another. Young describes this criticism in the following way:

> In this ideal each understands the others and recognizes the others in the same way that they understand themselves. This ideal thus submits to what Derrida calls the metaphysics of presence, which seeks to collapse the temporal difference inherent in language and experience into a totality that can be comprehended in one view. This ideal community denies the ontological difference within and between subjects. (Young, 1990a: 231).

This disagreement remains at the heart of Young's most recent interactions with Benhabib. First, and more general, she claims that Benhabib's reliance on the notion of enlarged thought runs the high risk of "closing off differentiation among subjects that Benhabib wants to keep open" (Young, 1994: 167). This extends the earlier criticism of such a project because a notion like enlarged thinking, in Young's estimation, presupposes mirror sameness or most problematically the interchangeable nature of such subjects. It is a symmetrical view of subjects where "I project onto them a perspective that complements my own" (Young, 1994: 168-169). Instead of seeing ourselves as mirrored in others, Young begins by assuming that interaction means encountering otherness in a way that does not nor need not identify with their otherness.

> Different social positions encounter one another with the awareness of their difference. This does not mean that we believe we have no similarities; difference is not total otherness. But it means that each position is aware that it does not comprehend the perspective of the others differently located, in the sense that it cannot be assimilated into one's own. There is thus

something to be learned from the other's perspectives as they communicate their meanings and perspectives, precisely because the perspectives are beyond one another and not reducible to a common good (Young, 1996: 127).

Second, and more specifically, Young's criticism of Benhabib is that her position "wrongly reduces reciprocal recognition to an ontological concept of a reversibility of standpoints" (Young, 1994: 169). Young's claim, as we will see in a moment, is that no such reversibility is possible even if it is desirable. Related to this criticism is the overlooked yet significant dimension of privilege. Here Young takes issue with the so-called shared experiences of those engaging in reversibility. Any talk of reversibility assumes the equally legitimate nature of all perspectives and is not the case where structured social injustices exist (like racism, for example). What is more likely to occur in these cases is a reversibility with one whose shared experience and privilege is similar. Young concludes:

> The social fact of structural privilege and oppression...creates the possibility of a falsifying projection. . . . When members of privileged groups imaginatively try to represent to themselves the perspective of members of oppressed groups, too often those representations carry projections and fantasies through which the privileged reinforce a complementary image of themselves (Young, 1994: 171).

The result of Benhabib's view, third, is that instead of aiding the communicative process (something Young interprets Benhabib to be saying), such a view in fact impedes dialogical communication. Imagining or thinking you know how one feels can be detrimental to a dialogical encounter because if you have represented the other position to yourself then "you may not listen to their expressions of their perspectives very openly. If you think you can look at things from their points of view, then you may avoid the sometimes arduous and painful process in which they confront you with your prejudices, fantasies, and misunderstandings about them, which you have because of your point of view" (Young, 1994: 172). Finally, Young believes that Benhabib's proposal has no place for "care-taking, deferential, polite acknowledgment of the Otherness of others" (Ibid). More precisely, a symmetrical understanding of reciprocity does not allow for three important embodied components, greeting, rhetoric, and storytelling, which Young claims are essential for understanding reciprocity as asymmetrical. These three components, inspired by her own reading of Arendt, are vital because "they recognize the embodiment and particularity of interlocutors, these three modes of communication help establish and maintain the plurality that...is necessary to the meaning and existence of publicity" (Young, 1996: 129). Why is this necessary? Young concludes: "Since much democratic discussion will be fraught with disagreement, anger, conflict, counter argument, and criticism, intermittent gestures of flattery, greeting, deference, and conciliatory caring keep commitment to the discussion at times of anger and disagreement" (Young, 1996: 130).

Young's alternative, then, includes the following. First, like Benhabib, Young proposes an "egalitarian reciprocity," which depends more on differences than unity. As she says, "Understanding another social location can here mean that there has been successful expression of experience and perspective, so that other social positions learn, and part of what they understand is that there remains more behind that experience and perspective that transcends their own subjectivity" (Young, 1997: 128). Second, as I have indicated, her view of reciprocity is one of asymmetry instead of symmetry. As asymmetrical the reversibility of perspectives is denounced while reciprocality is retained. "The reciprocal recognition by which I know that I am other for you just as you are other for me," writes Young, "cannot entail a reversibility of perspectives, precisely because our positions are partly constituted by the perspectives each of us has of the others" (Young, 1994: 170). Finally, this alternative of asymmetrical reciprocity leaves open the possibility that things about the other will not be understood. The result, according to Young, will be the likelihood of being more open to listening to the expressions of their experience, interests, and claims.[6]

Benhabib's response to Young is essentially an elaboration of her earlier thoughts yet she has added new emphases. First, Benhabib reemphasizes the importance of embodiedness. I say re-emphasizes because in her book *Situating the Self* Benhabib argues for an embodied and embedded understanding of communicative ethics and criticizes disembodied and disembedded understandings that she rejects. However, Benhabib does not want to go as far as Young in privileging lived bodily experiences in guiding deliberative processes because, according to Benhabib, "Greeting, storytelling, and rhetoric, although they may be aspects of informal communication in our everyday life, cannot become the public language of institutions and legislatures in a democracy. . . ." (Benhabib, 1996b: 83). Second, Benhabib points out, and correctly I think, that Young mis-characterizes her position as one arguing solely for symmetrical reciprocity instead of asymmetrical reciprocity. Benhabib reminds Young that she never uses this language. In fact, Benhabib reemphasizes her own distinction between "formal" and "complementary" reciprocity, the former suggesting a more symmetrical relationship while the latter an asymmetrical one. Third, and what is more strongly stated in recent discussions, Benhabib claims that Young's position runs the risk of falling prey either to forms of "extreme nominalism" or "essentializing group identities." Instead of nominalism or group essentialism, Benhabib believes that taking seriously the reversibility of perspectives, via enlarged thinking, creates the possibility of transforming our already preconceived notions of certain issues. She concludes, "Precisely because reversibility of perspectives is possible, social learning around issues like sexism, racism, and ethnic discrimination is possible. Moral change and political transformation can only take place through learning to take the standpoint of the other into account" (Benhabib, 1994: 189).

I have taken this necessary detour through Arendt, Benhabib and Young to show not only the background of the debate on reversibility, but to help us see more clearly what a Merleau-Pontian account might offer. In short, the Benhabib-Young debate has revealed the horns of the dilemma, which threaten to undermine my efforts at reconsidering the utopian. On the one hand we need a view of reversibility that does not assume the transparency of selves, the tyranny of sameness (Young's concern and her subsequent proposal). On the other hand, we need a view of reversibility that does not lead to solipsism or nominalism, which causes potential paralysis and hinders our efforts at transformative politics (Benhabib's concern and proposal). My claim is that Merleau-Ponty's writing on reversibility can help us to negotiate this dilemma. After all, Merleau-Ponty was as concerned about reversing perspectives as much as Arendt and Benhabib. Like them, he believed that to fail in this regard meant to open the door for what he called "corruption." Writing in opposition to the colonization of Indochina in 1947, Merleau-Ponty states that "It is in a precise sense scandalous that a Christian should show himself so incapable of getting outside himself and his "ideas" and should refuse to see himself even for an instance through the eyes of others" (Merleau-Ponty, 1964b: 324).

Defining reversibility might seem to be an easy task. It both is and is not. It is seemingly an easy task because in many respects reversibility suggests a simple inversion of something similar. But insofar as it is more than a simple inversion of the same, reversibility is complicated. Thus, to get at a richer understanding let us consider the following components that can deepen our understanding of reversibility. Let me begin with some general remarks.

First, reversibility, that "ultimate truth" for Merleau-Ponty, evokes the idea of mutuality but not of complete and perfect mutuality (Merleau-Ponty, 1968: 155).[7] True, it is that which implies an interconnectedness of me with others where the other can refer to both the human and extra-human. Second, reversibility participates in what could be called the movement of transcendence, which is to say that the other "transcends me, for example, in such regional sameness as species likeness, communal likeness, addresses to me, or likenesses of occurrences" (Scott, 1997: 36). Because of this movement of transcendence summoned by reversibility, shared human experience, to the degree of either complete and fixed unity or unanimous consensus among us before agreement is possible, is problematized. What this movement of transcendence suggests, then, is that reversibility also means *withdrawal*. That is to say, the other is in a reversible stance from us in a sense of withdrawal insofar as we can never completely, exhaustively or transparently know the position of the other. And here is the understanding I believe to be lost when we bypass reversibility too quickly for reciprocity. As Merleau-Ponty writes, "I can count on what I see, which is in close correspondence with what the other sees . . . and yet at the same time *I never rejoin the other's lived experience*" (VI, 10). We never rejoin the other's lived experience because it always transcends us to the point that it withdraws itself from us. This point is worth pursuing.

Reversibility for Merleau-Ponty is located within the framework of what he calls "flesh." It has its roots, however, in the *Phenomenology of Perception* where he writes that my body "perceives the body of another, and discovers in that other body a miraculous prolongation of my own intentions, a familiar way of dealing with the world" (Merleau-Ponty, 1962: 354).[8] Such a remark foreshadows what Merleau-Ponty says throughout *The Visible and the Invisible* such as, for example, his claim that "My body is made of the same flesh as the world (it is a perceived), and moreover this flesh of my body is shared by the world, the world *reflects* it, encroaches upon it and it encroaches upon the world" (VI: 248).

Merleau-Ponty is clear that flesh is *not* to be understood as analogous to the flesh of our body. Even though the flesh of the world is not "*self-sensing* as is my flesh...I call it flesh nonetheless...in order to say that it is a *pregnancy* of possibles . . . . It is by the flesh of the world that in the last analysis one can understand the lived body (*corps propre*)"— (VI: 250). So, even though flesh is not modeled on our flesh, our flesh, nevertheless, participates in and influences universal flesh. That is, flesh is universal in the sense that it cannot be exhausted or subjugated to our experiences of it as an object and is why Merleau-Ponty can say that "the world *reflects* it, encroaches upon it and it encroaches upon the world."

What is suggested by the use of the word flesh as opposed to body is the idea that there is a pre-ontological dimension to embodiment; that is, a dimension that is pre-thematic and that in a pre-schematic way illuminates an ideal political community. David Michael Levin helpfully remarks that flesh articulates, however ambiguously, a new "historical project for the ontological truth of our incarnation as human beings" (Levin, 1985: 67). That is to say, flesh prepares or orients us in a primordial way that, in Levin's words, makes us ready for "the mutual recognitions in a primordial sociality and [makes us] ready for the mutual recognitions and reciprocities constitutive of a more mature social world, a moral and political community" (Levin, 1990: 42). As we see, flesh is linked to and derived from an examination of the body but is not to be understood *as* the flesh of our body (cf. VI: 136-137). Or, more correctly, our bodies are not flesh yet our bodies participate in universal flesh, which means that our bodies are present to flesh insofar as they are, at a certain level, similar "stuff." Without this commonality, something Young tends to overlook, nothing would be there. Flesh, then, signifies commonality in which our bodies participate. Thus, flesh possesses both a corporeal and an incorporeal significance, which Merleau-Ponty describes in the following way.

> [F]lesh is not matter, in the sense of corpuscles of being which would add up or continue on one another to form beings. . . . The flesh is not matter, is not mind, is not substance. To designate it we should need the old term "element," in the sense it was used to speak of water, air, earth, and fire, that is, in the sense of a *general thing*, midway between the spatio-temporal individual and the idea, a sort of incarnate principle that brings a style of being wherever there is a fragment of being (VI: 139).

Said differently, flesh is that which "extends further than the things I touch and see at present." Flesh is "there" and announces how we not only exist in a social world but how this social world also dwells in us via our participation in universal flesh (VI: 143). In this regard, we could say that flesh has a texture, but a texture understood as intertwinement or reversibility; a reversibility always imminent and never realized in fact.[9]

Let me put this discussion more directly in terms of reversibility. Our participation in and through flesh, links us to others in a way that cannot reduce them to our own hermeneutical frameworks, that is, make them as unfamiliar threats familiar extensions of ourselves. Moreover, our participation in universal flesh means that we do not act in isolation because, as bodies (in the *Phenomenology of Perception*) and bodies-as-flesh (in *The Visible and the Invisible*), we are intercorporeally linked with each other which means that our actions, movements or visions concerning society "touch" others as much as theirs "touch" us. Let me elaborate.

First, flesh, like embodiment in the *Phenomenology of Perception*, is a phenomenological concept but not a biological one, which means that, among other things, it resists being reduced to a category whereby we explain our relationship to it in terms of causality. As a phenomenological concept, flesh pays attention to and resonates with the body of lived experience (cf. Levin, 1985: 330). Second, flesh illuminates our common intercorporeality so that we can think both identity and difference. In this regard, flesh is nothing other than a label for that most basic problem running throughout the history of philosophy: "the problem of sameness and otherness, of identity and difference, of the One and the same" (Madison, 1990: 29). Put in more political terms, flesh orders our thinking about society—i.e., how it might be, or could be—more in terms of becoming rather than actuality. Thus, flesh is not some kind of telic principle that constitutes or even regulates our experience of it. To the contrary, flesh as a "wild being" or "general thing" problematizes any once-and-for-all positing of trans-historical, dis-embodied visions of our life together and instead, presents our co-existence together as that which organically unfolds in the manner of life itself, first in lived bodily experience and now in universal flesh. Third, flesh is universal insofar as it gestures more fully toward that dimension which ontologically, or better pre-ontologically, orients us and enables us to act in harmony—not a harmony in which otherness is reduced to sameness, but harmony where the Other always transcends us; a transcendence characterized as alterity. It is a harmony that illuminates the possibility of something rather than nothing. In a word, flesh is that "stuff" which keeps us together and at the same time keeps us apart. It is in this regard that flesh can be thought of as a non-orderly order by which I mean the following.

On the one hand, flesh is a "being in latency" (VI: 136), a "sort of incarnate principle" (VI: 139) that is "not contingency, or chaos, but a texture that returns to itself and conforms to itself" (VI: 146). It is a texture that generates intercorporeity. On the other hand, flesh is a "wild being" and has "no name in traditional philosophy to designate it," (VI: 139) which means that it cannot be reduced to some kind of eidetic principle that keeps Otherness always in the cross-hairs of sameness. There is an order to flesh but an order that does not express rigid control and mastery over Otherness. Instead, it is an order that illuminates a primordial energy that empowers us to act in an intertwining manner whereby we find ourselves living in the facial expressions of the other (and he or she in mine). Flesh is that which reveals reversibility because flesh is, in Merleau-Pontian terms, another way of thinking about "the system of 'me-and-other'" (Merleau-Ponty, 1964b: 146).

Above I said that as participants in universal flesh we "touch" each other with our actions, movements and ideas. I say this because the understanding of reversibility I am suggesting here, following Merleau-Ponty, is an asymmetrical understanding that is best understood on the model of one hand touching the other (VI: 39). For example, it is not the same whenever I touch myself as when another touches me. To be sure, these two experiences of touching are not dissimilar; neither do they coincide. As reversible there is similarity between these experiences but not sameness: Similarity within asymmetry. Further, it indicates the inability of one hand to completely coincide with the other. This means that the reversibility of flesh is not about complete self-transparency between subjects, for this would mean falling into what Merleau-Ponty calls the thesis of "coincidence." And because Merleau-Ponty affirms a thesis of "non-coincidence," there is always a distance between the other and me that cannot in the end be overcome by virtue of our singular locations. This means that, first, we can never know completely what the other feels because we are not they and they are not we, just as my one hand touching the other can never know completely what the other hand feels. Second, because Merleau-Ponty's reversibility is hermeneutically informed he is aware that in interpreting the other we can never understand his or her intentions in a transparent fashion, much in the same way, we can never exhaust the interpretation of a text. There is always a distance between the other and me. This does not mean, to be sure, that we cannot enter into the world of the other, an insight not lost on either Arendt or Merleau-Ponty. Rather, it means, in a positive manner, that in our efforts to know the Other in his or her singularity there will be, to invoke an idea from Paul Ricoeur, a "surplus of meaning," which is to say that the Other as transcendent always escapes our attempts to represent them transparently, and this surplus of meaning insures that the interpretive process remains alive (cf. Ricoeur, 1976). This is what I take Merleau-Ponty to mean when he says that we borrow from the other, take from or encroach upon the other, and intersect with the other in a way that is chiasmic. Once again, touch is the model where things "touch me as I touch them and touch myself: flesh of the world—distinct from my flesh: the double inscription outside and inside. The inside receives without flesh: not a "psychic state," but intra-corporeal, reverse of the outside that my body shows to the things" (VI: 261).

Understood in this light, to speak of reversing perspectives is to signify our intercorporeality, modeled on touching, as that which makes possible the illumination of the pre-social and pro-moral quality of flesh and body-as-flesh. It speaks of an intercorporeality defined by intertwining and reversibility, one modeled on a primordial understanding of the body-as-flesh. This is why, as the condition for seeing and being seen, touching and being touched, hearing and being heard, the reversibility of flesh motivates us to illuminate more fully the outlines that already socially attune us to a concealed ideal of intercorporeal subjects (cf. VI: 148 and Levin, 1988: 333).

We can conclude from the above discussion that, first, as a medium, flesh locates us within a particular framework. Second, the reversibility of flesh as the "flesh of the world" is "a *pregnancy* of possibles," which means that flesh at least indicates the potential to intertwine our becoming together, what Merleau-Ponty refers to as intercorporeity. Insofar as we participate in flesh we apprehend, albeit briefly, the ideal community of intercorporeal beings (VI: 250). It is for these reasons that I believe that the reversibility of flesh, while not receiving extensive delineation in Merleau-Ponty's political writings, is, nevertheless, shot through with political overtones. Consider, for example, a comment he makes in *Humanism and Terror*. He says, "To understand and judge a society, one has to penetrate its basic structure to the human bond upon which it is built; this undoubtedly depends upon legal relations, but also upon forms of labor, ways of loving, living, and dying" (Merleau-Ponty, 1969: xiv). That which is prior to the legal relations and orients our relationships characterized by love, life, and dying are other ways of thinking about our participation in universal flesh. There is, in short, reversibility here: "each the other side of the other" (VI: 263). So, flesh, we might say in this respect, is a "surface" in that it allows for diverse values and commitments. Thus, borrowing a thought from Charles Scott, flesh can be thought of as "the space of 'the' people in the sense that the multiplicity, divergence, and struggle of individuals is maximized rather than a unity of the principles and values that regulate people and make them appear as 'one.' By acting and thinking in reference to such space one is able to engage practices and discourses, not in the name of 'higher' values but by focusing attention 'on the realities that have gone unnoticed' and by showing 'what is intolerable and what it is in an intolerable situation that makes it truly intolerable'" (Scott, 1997: 184). How, then, does this notion of reversibility I am employing from Merleau-Ponty relate to the insistence on the primacy of reciprocity in most political ethics of our day?

Let me begin this final section by indicating how I understand reciprocity. To reciprocate is first to recognize you as worthy of a response. Reciprocity, then, is a *decision*. In a moment of indecision I decide to recognize you as someone with whom I am intertwined and with whom I could relate through my response to you. Thus, to reciprocate is to reflect this intertwinement through my response

toward you that is an ethic, a way of comporting myself toward you
in the response. Reciprocity is *not* that which makes my decision
to reciprocate possible. It is the response to you that illuminates an
always-already condition of being-with-you, which is the condition of
reversibility as flesh as outlined above. Reciprocity, therefore, requires,
or better presupposes reversibility. To say that reciprocity is a response
that reflects this condition of reversibility is to say, further, that
reciprocity is a *particular kind* of response to reversibility.

Reciprocity, then, illuminates this condition of reversibility in a
way that reflects our being-together toward a future. Reciprocity, as that
which takes seriously the otherness of those we encounter, is, for lack
of a better word, a positive response to this condition of reversibility. It
is a response that, upon realizing the reversible stance we find ourselves
in, can make us alter our course of action. Reciprocity, following
Arendt's account of the story, is what Anton Schmidt employed in
the service of saving Jews from Hitler's death camps, but one made
possible because of the condition he found himself in with Jews being
murdered, a condition of reversibility(See Arendt 1963: 230).

The point I am emphasizing here is that our choice to reciprocate
is possible only because I find myself in a condition by which I can
reverse perspectives with you, a condition for our being-together.
While this may be a contestable point, I remain convinced, following
Merleau-Ponty, that reversibility, however, is *not* yet an ethical
stance. It is, rather, the condition for my ethical (non)response.
Neither is it a cognitive capacity that we all share that, with proper
activation, enables us to respond accordingly. And here we see how
a phenomenologically grounded account of reversibility differs from
Benhabib's Habermasian communicative account. Reversibility is
not something I *do*; neither is it a procedural apparatus that *ensures*
we will respond ethically. Rather, reversibility is the condition for the
possibility *of* the doing, it is the condition for the possibility *of* the
procedure, which in this case is the choice of reciprocity. And this
condition, as I have been developing it from Merleau-Ponty, is *both*
the condition for being-together *and* being-apart, which is to say it is a
condition that can either be illuminated or deadened. The condition of

reversibility, then, is the condition for the response in general and the ethical response in particular.

I can respond in a way that reveals this condition as a condition for our flourishing. I can, equally through my choice not to reciprocate, conceal this condition, which is the condition that keeps us apart. And the reality is that we do not always act in ways that illuminate reversibility whereby reciprocity is possible. As Eichmann illustrates, I may respond in a way that deadens this condition and decide you are unworthy of recognition and worthy of death. We could, for instance, argue that Eichmann did not possess the *capacity* to reverse perspectives, as does Arendt and Benhabib following her. In not "thinking from the standpoint of the other" Eichmann was deficient in some way, perhaps cognitively or imaginatively. This explanation, a viable one I think, still nevertheless makes reversibility something we *do*, namely, imaginatively leap to the others' position so that we "see" their suffering and respond in a way that does not kill them. It further makes the choice of reversing, through an imaginative leap to the other, a potentially violent move where we *make* the other who is unfamiliar familiar. In this case, then, Young's criticisms are correct.

On the other hand, if reversibility is the condition for the possibility of Eichmann's decision either to reciprocate or not, Eichmann, on my Merleau-Pontian reading, is *still* in a condition of reversibility with those whose death he commissioned. His response is one that refuses this condition, rejects its possibility for being-together and as a result refuses the condition of reversibility. We could further speculate that Eichmann did in fact recognize the place of the other, put himself in their shoes, so to speak, and *still* decide to kill them. His response, in this case, would be one that does not extend reciprocity but rather refuses it *based on* the condition that he, as Nazi, finds himself in with Jews who are other, and whom he decides are not worthy of the title "human." His *decision* to carry out the killings is a choice *not* to reciprocate but a choice that is still possible because of the condition of reversibility, in this case a reversible stance he refuses to illuminate and instead deaden. In the end, the way we comport ourselves toward the other, whether in ways that help us flourish, or ways that violate us, is possible because of the condition of reversibility. This, as I have argued above, is one of the principal insights of Merleau-Ponty's notion of reversibility and how it might be extended to the question of reciprocity.

In sum, I have argued that Merleau-Ponty's notion of reversibility is important for two reasons. First, it is the condition for a being together, which is a condition for ethical relation itself. This means that reversibility functions in a critical manner, something with which philosophers like Benhabib are rightfully concerned. Second, his account helps us to understand that the condition we find ourselves in enables us to choose or respond to each other in ways that are asymmetrically reciprocal, even if and when those ways might inflict violence. The point here is that both are choices made possible by the condition of reversibility, and both responses are equally possible. This condition of reversibility, from a Merleau-Pontian perspective, is one that does not assume a completely mutual understanding but recognizes the other in a way that can understand their sufferings so that in our response we can choose to recognize this otherness and not eradicate it (something feminist philosophers have shown convincingly). In the end, Merleau-Ponty enables us to confront constructively the problems of radical individual nominalism or detrimental group essentialism, one a concern of Young, the other a potential implication of her rejection of reversibility. The structure of reversibility, developed within the framework of Merleau-Pontian universal flesh, speaks clearly to the fact that we are inhabited by and inhabit a common world. As an adventure in common pursuits, structured by the reversibility of flesh, this means that our intertwinement is a dialectical co-inhabiting whereby we always struggle to resist the extremes of the implications of any discussion of reversibility: On the one hand, the notion of reversibility as withdrawal means that we can never fully join ourselves, or better, join the other to ourselves. This distance, this remaining apart, is a key feature to the way reversibility structures our collective actions, which is to say it reminds us not only how group essentialism eradicates particularity and otherness, but also that we are incapable, ultimately, of producing the harmony envisioned in virtually all utopian projects. Reversibility, in this way, reminds us that we are forever separated. On the other hand, reversibility reminds us that we are held together by the commonality that is "flesh." As such, reversibility reminds us that despite our calls for embodiedness, which is a way of emphasizing the particularity of our lives, we are finally collectively bound to and with each other. As he Merleau-Ponty knew, we could *never* in a transparent manner subsume the other under the same because "our situations cannot be superimposed on each other" (PP, 356). This leads him to conclude:

> If, moreover, we undertake the same project in common, this common project is not one single project, it does not appear in the selfsame light to both of us, we are not both equally enthusiastic about it, or at any rate not in quite the same way, simply because Paul is Paul and I am myself. Although his consciousness and mine, working through our respective situations, may contrive to produce a common situation in which they can communicate, it is nevertheless from the subjectivity of each of us that each one projects this "one and only" world (Ibid).

This passage provides a good transition to the final section of this chapter. In what follows I juxtapose the conceptual work done in the previous sections with the vision of coalition politics offered by Bernice Johnson Reagon. What we will see is how reversibility in the Merleau-Pontian sense of the word as that which simultaneously separates and holds us together, structures the politics of utopian possibility as instanced by Reagon and others who engage in such politics .

Reagon's notion of coalition politics, I suggest, embodies the Merleau-Pontian idea of flesh and the idea of reversibility entailed by it (Reagon, 1983).[10] As such, reversibility as an element of the utopian enables transformative political activity among groups that come from different locations, groups whose identities are often radically opposed and incommensurable, and groups whose sensibilities, understandings, and relationships with power are diverse. These people who are Other and different to one another need each other, influence each other because people who are subjugated in diverse ways need each other in order to survive. What holds them together despite the fact that their subjugation is different and Other is, to borrow Merleau-Ponty's words, their "common situation in which they can communicate," namely, their need for survival. The potential for liberation, however, is more than a need for survival. It is that which survives us which, for her is "the principles that are the basis of your practice" (366). Now, her language of "principles" here might get our anti-foundational dander up. I submit, however, that her claims of "principles that are the basis of your practice" is another way of extending Merleau-Ponty's idea of the reversibility of flesh. How so? First, her principles draw us together in ways that allow us to encounter others as Other, acknowledging their transcendence to us, and thereby opening us onto the world toward new understandings and possibilities. Via these principles we begin to be aware that all people's struggle against subjugation is done so in specific locations and through multiple avenues. Thus, while these principles let groups who are other and different struggle for liberation in their own spaces, they still function in her thought in such a way that empower us to transcend those articulations of identity—ontological, political, ethical or otherwise—that can trap us in fixed essentialist identifications, traps that can lead to political paralysis instead of political transformation. Reagon echoes this when, speaking to a "Woman-Identified" conference, she says:

> We've pretty much come to the end of a time when you can have a space that is "yours only"—just for the people you want to be there. Even when we have our "women-only" festivals, there is no such thing. The fault is not necessarily with the organizers of the gathering. To a large extent it's because we have just finished with that kind of isolating. There is no hiding place. There is nowhere you can go and only be with people who are like you. It's over. Give it up (357).

Now, Reagon may be overstating her case in that there may in fact be plenty of places you can go to be with people who are like you, graduate school, church, synagogue, mosque, or temple. Her point, a Merleau-Pontian one I believe, is a subtle one. While you may think you are with those only like yourself, you, your cohorts and the actions that govern you have a way of "touching" everyone, in this case those you seek to keep outside of the barred rooms you build. Reagon's way of explaining what Merleau-Ponty calls the system of the me-and-other, understood as reversibility of flesh, is to say that "There is no chance you can survive by staying *inside* the barred room." (358). Now recall that as participants in universal flesh, we cannot escape the reversibility that links our actions. Remember, for Merleau-Ponty "There is no For Itself and For the Other. They are each the other side of the other" (VI 263). No matter how hard we try to isolate ourselves, at some point universal flesh, the wild-being that it is with its pregnant possibilities, comes calling to remind us that we are "intercorporeal beings, . . . which extends further than the things I touch and see at present" (VI, 143). In this regard, the wild being of flesh makes us uncomfortable, but an unsettling that opens us to transformative possibilities. Here is Reagon's way of helping us understand the wild being of universal flesh.

> Sometimes you get comfortable in your little barred room. And you decide you in fact going to live there and carry out all of your stuff in there. And you gonna take care of everything that needs to be taken care of in the barred room. If you're white and in the barred room and if everybody's white, one of the first things you try to take care of is making sure that people don't think that the barred room is a racist barred room. So you begin to talk about racism and the first thing you do is say, "Well, maybe we better open the door and let some Black folks in the barred room." Then you think, "Well, how we gonna figure out whether they're X's or not?" Because there's nothing in the room but X's. You go down the checklist. You been working a while to sort our who you are, right? So you go down the checklist and say, "If we can find Black folk like that we'll let them in the room." You don't really want Black folks, you are just looking for yourself with a little color to it.

The first thing that happens is that the room don't feel like the room anymore. (Laughter) And it ain't home no more. It is not a womb no more. And you can't feel comfortable no more. And what happened at that point has to do with trying to do too much in it. You don't do no coalition building in a womb. It's just like trying to get a baby used to taking a drink when they're in your womb. It just doesn't work too well. Inside the womb you generally are very soft and unshelled. You have no covering. And you have no ability to handle what happens if you start to let folks in who are not like you.

Coalition work is not work done in your home (359ff).

Merleau-Ponty's reversibility of flesh as an element for thinking about the utopian strikes me in a similar fashion. As an in-between it helps us to think identity and difference, sameness and otherness. As participants in universal flesh who always touch those with whom we are different and other, we cannot live in a way that does not touch another. The wild-being never rests. As en-fleshed bodies who touch others who are different and are touched by them, our locations effect those who are other to us and to whom we are other. What becomes apparent, from both Merleau-Ponty and Reagon, is that political efforts structured by the reversibility of flesh involves a risk insofar as we do not know in advance how we will adjudicate the best approaches to our political efforts. But we can say something, I believe, about how we proceed in such a way that holds together otherness and communion.

To aid us in this let me return to Bernice Reagon's claim that in coalition politics "Most of the time you feel threatened to the core and if you don't, you're not really doing no coalescing" (356). I take her here to be saying that if we are really concerned with doing transformative politics then we better be aware that those with whom we transform might be so different and other that we fear them, despise them, or even hate them. Reagon's remark can be read as one that acknowledges the importance of interpretation for reversibility, something I will discuss in terms of the "hermeneutics of testimony" in the following chapter.

To conclude, I want to draw together more concisely the connections between what I have been discussing and the way this relates to the utopian. To begin with, let me say that the structure of the reversibility of flesh as it relates to the utopian can be understood as an extension of the structures of embodiment discussed in the previous chapter. Like the structures of embodiment, the reversibility of flesh is that which loosens us up for something different, something that, as wholly other, interrupts our determinate horizons of lived experience. As a condition that discloses to us the other as wholly other, the reversibility of flesh provides a critical dimension to the movement of the utopian because it possesses the capability of radically calling into question the horizon of existence in which we become, epistemically, ethically and politically. The very structure of this reversibility as the reversibility of flesh is the structure of the utopian itself, in that it breaks into and upsets the flow of our attempts to ground our understanding of ourselves, others and the world through the horizon of sameness, a sameness that ultimately erases particularity. Though it need not always be the case, reversibility of flesh as the structure of utopian thinking loosens us from the premature move to close off or encircle the other within the same. Note however, this is not to deny the possibility of shared experiences. Neither, as we will see more in the following chapter, is this to suggest that utopian thinking lacks a universal intent. Instead, it is to reject a particular understanding of shared experiences that requires we acknowledge them beforehand in order to procure agreement. It is thinking which resists the homogenizing of otherness into sameness so that a prediction can be given of how things are or will be. Put in Merleau-Ponty's terms it is to say that to the degree that the utopian is structured by the reversibility of flesh the utopian participates in the intertwining of ourselves and the other; a relationship that cannot always have laid out in advanced the principles that reflect a "common human understanding." This reversibility of flesh as a structure of the utopian exposes us and makes us vulnerable to the multiple voices in need of hearing; a vulnerability that is, to be sure, risky, but one that in its risk keeps the event of utopian thinking moving and helps in preventing the closing off of future horizons.

What the structure of reversibility offers to utopian thinking, then, is the following. First, linked to active transcendence, reversibility, as that which simultaneously separates and binds, illuminates for us the idea of movement without which any clear and distinct destination is made possible. As that which is structured by reversibility of flesh and elucidated by our encounters with the other, the utopian is not the capacity to see clearly and distinctly. Instead, the utopian is that which moves dialectically between the incarnate, embodied ground of the utopian and universal spirit of the utopian as that which collectively, at its best, binds us together, in effect putting an end to any thought that the body is yet another foundation upon which we can guarantee being-together. Second, reversibility of flesh gives us no assurances that we are on the right track; only that we are intertwined with the other in this movement so that our visions are affected by them and affect them in rudimentary ways. Third, as the reversibility of flesh which speaks of movement in relationship with and to the other, the utopian is fueled by the passion that resides in our commonality, a commonality that cannot, because of the separating power of reversibility be enacted once-and-for-all, but a commonality that still, because of the binding power of reversibility, reminds us that our futures are always intertwined.

To sum up, and to paraphrase Merleau-Ponty, the ideality of something like what we will see in the utopian politics of the South African Truth and Reconciliation Commission in the final chapter is one grounded in the bodily existence of all—victims, victimizers, other South Africans— an "ideal community of embodied subjects," but is also an ideality that is not alien to universal flesh which "gives it its axes, its depth" (VI, 152). Recall that flesh in general and participation in universal flesh in particular is that which accomplishes this and contributes significantly to utopian as "a *pregnancy* of possibles." Merleau-Ponty helps to bring together my argument in this chapter (as well as the previous one) in his remarks in the "Working Note" mentioned earlier where he says the following:

Flesh of the world, described (apropos of time, space, movement) as segregation, dimensionality, continuation, latency, encroachment.... . That means that my body is made of the same flesh as the world (it is a perceived), and moreover that this flesh of my body is shared by the world, the world *reflects* it, encroaches upon it and it encroaches upon the world . . . , they are in a relation of transgression or of overlapping—This also means: my body is not only one perceived among others, it is the measurant (*mesurant*) of all, *Nullpunkt*, of all the dimensions of the world (VI, 248-249).

The reversibility of flesh attunes the utopian thought toward logic that is pre-thematically lived rather than determined. Such an attunement does not, however, mean that the utopian structured now by embodiment and reversibility lacks the critical capacity to make claims on either us or those with whom we are intertwined. To the contrary, the utopian, with the element of reversibility now seen in the light the above, is precisely the return of the universal, albeit in a different manner. It is, in short, a universal that emerges in the particular, a universal that while retaining the truthfulness of the utopian (ad)event cannot be made clear and distinct, but rather is that to which we can only witness. Witnessing, or bearing testimony to the utopian becomes a separate element. How we understand what it means to give testimony to the utopian and act as a responsible witness requires its own discussion.

Chapter Five

Witnessing to the Utopian

In this chapter I turn to the final element in my understanding of the utopian, the element of testimony or witnessing. What I want to develop more carefully is the idea that we seek to become responsible witnesses to the encounter that has transformed our thought. This thought is where we begin to make transitions from "historically defined positions, through contemporaneously improvised dramas, and towards a future immanent in the momentum of the moment yet in manifest and subtle ways discontinuous and thus surprising" (Colapietro, 1998: 130). Moreover, we attempt to witness to this new thought through responsible action(s). In this light, my thesis is that a witness to the utopian will be one who practices responsible testimony. This requires explaining what I mean by testimony and how I use it, as well as clarifying the characteristics of a witness who is responsible. I will begin by discussing testimony.

First, there is the character of testimony. Just as I suggested for the idea of the utopian in Chapter One, there exists both a colloquial and technical understanding of testimony. The colloquial understanding, what might be called "ordinary testimony," is rooted in the idea that to give testimony is simply to recount an experience of something, i.e., to give a version of an experience or event of which one is directly a part. This is what Paul Ricoeur calls the "quasi-empirical" dimension of testimony because it "is not perception itself but the report, the story, the narration of the event" (Ricoeur, 1980: 123). A witness in a trial best illustrates this colloquial understanding. Witnesses testify, which is to say they tell their story. But a witness does more than this. A witness who gives an account of a certain experience makes a claim against another potentially conflicting account(s). Second, testimony is heard or seen (either directly or indirectly). Testimony joins one to others insofar as in the recounting it makes claims on and to those who listen, argues for an account and seeks to convince others of its veracity. Even an act of ordinary testimony attempts to construct reality based on a particular experience, an account that is always in contention. After all, not all testimony is equal. There is false testimony. What is important, which applies to false testimony as well, is that testimony is an act designed to convince, convert, prove, or otherwise, and most often has as its goal the construction of reality based on the experience of an event. Again, a witness in a trial serves as a good example. To testify is to attest to something but is also to testify for or in favor of that which one has been called to give an account (cf. Ricoeur, 1980: 124). In this light, third, testimony is at the service of judgment and allows us to measure the utopian encounter against other possibilities. I will return to this theme below in different ways, but here I want to say that even at this colloquial level testimony already raises issues that will become significant for elaborating the characteristics of a responsible witness (i.e., truthfulness and critical judgment).

Now that we have seen the roots of the colloquial understanding, let me offer a more technical understanding that I employ. I want to begin by claiming there is first order testimony, which reveals the event and our immediate encounter to it. The witness is a witness *to* the event but is also confronted *by* the event. In other words, borrowing an idea from Ricoeur, being a witness in this first-order sense is both *to interpret and be interpreted* by the event that has interrupted us. Something occurs. It lays a claim on us. We then seek to understand this encounter, which is to say interpret it. In this way, the encounter is interpreted but in doing so we become interpreted by the event, which we would describe perhaps as being transformed by it.

There is also a second-order testimony. The witness to the event is a witness to a witness of the event. In short, we often provide testimony not to the direct encounter, but to the encounter through someone or something else that is perhaps a witness to the initial event. In this way, we witness to a witness. This does not preclude the interruptive element of the utopian. To the contrary, we can become just as disrupted from a witness to the witness. Our testimony, therefore, will be to the original encounter not necessarily witnessed by us, but to the original encounter as others witness it. We still provide testimony to the original moment, in a first order way, only we do so as others transmit it, in a second order fashion. Either way, we witness to the utopian as we witness to the witness(es). Let me offer what might be a rather naïve example to elaborate this point.

First, I was not born when Martin Luther King delivered his "I Have a Dream Speech," nor was I able to see him achieve firsthand the political transformations while he was alive. It would, however, be difficult to deny that I have been unable to hear his recorded speeches or, more importantly, unable to hear *about* the numerous accounts, conflicting as they might be, of those who were (and were not) eyewitnesses. My own understanding of this movement, second, has been significantly formed as a result of hearing those who may or may not have been present at King's many deeds, but who have nonetheless undergone a transformation and are now witnesses to this event. These witnesses to King and the civil rights movement were key figures in the interruption of some of my early views about race relations and what it means to be black (and white) in the United States. Would we dare say that those who did not "see" King yet who "heard" his message through the telling and retelling, are any less capable of potentially communicating the ethical, political, and utopian import of his work? My answer, based on what I say above, is no. There are witnesses to the original event, and there are witnesses to the witnesses. The testimony we provide is to the witnesses (in a second order manner), but equally to the original utopian moment (in a first order manner).

The work of testimony in this example is that of the first and second order described above, and the utopian demand that things be different is carried through this second order witness that I expressed. Moreover, something else emerges here that is important to the element of witnessing to the utopian. This is that even though the utopian moment is always contextual it nonetheless carries with it *universal* intent. I will discuss this more below, but here I want to say that this intent always emerges from a particular experience and cannot ever be repeated exactly like the originary moment of disruption. This does not, as we will see, undermine the universal intent of the claims made on others (e.g., "Racism is wrong, everywhere" as a utopian demand from the Civil Rights movement); instead, it serves to remind us that a notion of the utopian that avoids becoming like traditional ones will shun making the move that says something like "Racism is wrong, everywhere, *and* the policy or program from this situation may serve to guide *all* situations, regardless of context." While the latter might still carry with it intent, it moves from intent to ultimate certainty that I have already suggested makes the utopian irrelevant in its theoretical abstraction. In the end, to witness to the utopian in the way I am describing it here means that the witness—either as a witness to the event itself or a witness to the witness as in the case of King and others—engages in the act of interpretation toward ourselves and to others.

A witness gives something to be interpreted in offering a testimony. We provide an interpretation of the event that we have undergone. Moreover, we attempt to make sense of this event relative to the experience of our particular situations. Thus, this attempt is an individual project where the interruptive demand to be interpreted is an act of self-understanding. However, as we saw in Chapter Four, we do not come to the utopian solely by turning inward to self-examination. Rather, the utopian demand by which we are interpreted in a way that is *self*-understanding demands to be interpreted in a *social* context. The interpretive demand is, therefore, double: to be interpreted by and interpret, the latter of which requires a social context. In this way, interpretation in a social context keeps the utopian moving. An act of giving testimony the utopian operates on the logic of "gift exchange" as opposed to an economy of exchange (Hyde, 1983).

According to this logic, interpretation that accompanies testimony is "erotic property" is able to keep the story of the occurrence of the utopian "on the move," or always becoming. Conversely, thought that cannot or does not move "loses its gift properties" and therefore loses its transformative capacity. Hyde explains the kind of movement I want to extend to the utopian in the following way.

The gift becomes an agent of social cohesion, and this again leads to the feeling that its passage increases its worth, for in social life, at least, the whole really is greater than the sum of its parts. If it brings the group together, the gift increases in worth immediately upon its first circulation, and then, like a faithful lover, continues to grow through constancy (Hyde, 1983: 8; 35).

In the context of what I have been saying, testimony to the utopian understood as "erotic property," means the following. First, the ability to keep open the space for transformation relies on the imaginative ability to create spaces in which the remembered yet hidden potential of the utopian makes politics about "unkept promises of the historical past being re-projected, reanimated in terms of a better future which might realize such lost opportunities or unfulfilled, betrayed, possibilities" (Hyde, 1983: 8). Even though Hyde uses the language of possibility here, it is better understood as potential in the way I have been suggesting. The point is that the utopian is always on the move, and such movement allows the utopian potential that is betrayed in stasis to be potentially brought to light. Second, as we will see more fully below with integrative feminisms, testimony as erotic property is another way of pointing out how shared experiences open us onto the world rather than close us off from it. To the degree that we can speak of shared experiences, however, it would be under the sign of reversibility as discussed in the previous chapter and not reciprocity. It is risking our very existence in the name of something that, in its arresting and interruptive power, we believe is better and that which binds us together as it keeps us apart. It is here, third, where critical judgment begins to emerge as a component of testimony. Whereas testimony is a gift that requires interpretation, testimony to the utopian as universal carries with it a *judgment*. As a gift, testimony establishes a relationship between existing parties. Testimony, moreover, has as one of its intended aims the normative judgment of visions that are under the critical eye of the utopian. In short, testimony "wants to justify, to prove the good basis of an assertion which, beyond the fact, claims to attain its meaning" (Ricoeur, 1980: 123–124).

The witness to the utopian is one who by virtue of giving a testimony to that which calls into question the current view of something, offers a judgment to the conditions that hide, truncate or diminish the utopian potential. Even in Chapter Three where I described the normative component of the utopian as experienced via bodily interactions, we saw with the illustration of Sojourner Truth how bodily interactions situated in a particular degrading context illuminate alternatives that carry with them normative weight against the current state of things. A testimony to this alternative in both thought and action is a critical act, by which I mean that testimony to the utopian judges the anti-utopian or the ideological as lacking the resources by which we can experience the utopian. Testimony to the transformative component of the utopian makes a claim on and to the particular degrading situations and those who embrace it. To put this straightforward, to witness to the utopian in this manner is to do so with *universal intent*.[1]

I say "universal intent," in general, to state that the utopian is not a wholesale acceptance that all the ways of being human is morally and politically valid. The utopian as a demand that things be different challenges the situatedness in the name of an emancipatory alternative claimed or thought to be relevant to *all*. In particular, I use this phrase to specify how an alternative notion of universal works in concert with my unconventional account of the utopian. What, then, is the nature of the kind of universal intent, and how do we arrive at it?

The Western philosophical tradition in general has been preoccupied with two primary tasks: (1) locating a point of reference that is context-independent in order to judge rival claims and (2) securing foundations upon which to ground philosophical systems. Such obsessions summarily describe conventional understandings of universalism.

The traditional understanding of universalism possesses the following characteristics. First, it views reason as a natural disposition of the mind, which assumes that all humans are like-minded creatures and able to discern proper truths that are thought to be clear and distinct. This traditional version of universalism, moreover, is substitutionalist because it assumes that the experiences of particular humans are representative of humans in general. Traditional universalism assumes that humans are like "geometricians in different rooms who, reasoning alone for themselves, all arrive at the same solution to a problem" (Benhabib, 1992: 163).

Second, this view of universalism relies on the existence of an Archimedean point of reference that is ahistorical and context-independent. Real knowledge on this view is universally fixed, timeless, and not contaminated by historical contingencies. Moral and political theory based on such a view is concerned primarily with finding these fixed universals as a way to unify contentious particulars. The result, so the argument goes, is a universalism capable of legislating among differences and able to procure total agreement. We can begin to see that an understanding of utopian thought generated from these notions would be one where uniformity, perfection, and unanimity are preeminent traits, all of which support the conventional notion of the utopian.

The language of traditional universalism corresponds to conventional understandings of objectivism, which Richard Bernstein helpfully describes in the following way.

> By 'objectivism' I mean the basic conviction that there is or must be some permanent, ahistorical matrix or framework to which we can ultimately appeal in determining the nature of rationality, knowledge, truth, reality, goodness, or rightness.... The objectivist maintains that unless we can ground philosophy, knowledge, or language in a rigorous manner we cannot avoid radical skepticism (Bernstein, 1983: 8).

In other words, like legislative universalism, objectivism centers on the notion that a "God's-eye-view" exists, one that transcends our contingent situations and provides a universally, non-culturally conditioned, reflective stance. Moreover, like traditional notions of universalism, objectivism claims that this point of reference is available to every rational being and must be assented to in order for there to be agreement. The implication is that without such agreement there exists nothing but radical relativism. This leads to the following results. First, subtle arguments are employed that seek out ever new ways to ground logic, science, philosophy, religion, morality, politics, social theory, or whatever else seems threatened. Second, this objectivist conception of rationality yields a grand either/or. Either there exists a fixed foundation upon which we can guarantee truth and action, or we are doomed to nihilistic relativism. This grand either/or of objectivism, third, radically reshapes conceptions of meaning so that it becomes viewed as an abstract relation where certain representations "mirror" an objective, mind-independent reality. In addition, as with the substitutionalist approach to universalism, this view assumes that "human beings can somehow 'plug into' a transcendent, autonomous rationality that stands beyond all historical developments" (Johnson, 1987: xxv). From the above discussion, then, we can see how an alternative understanding of universalism (as well as objectivity) is needed so that our particular situations are not ignored. Seyla Benhabib provides such a view. With regards to traditional legislative universalism she says "These are the illusions of a self transparent and self-grounding reason, the illusion of a disembedded and disembodied subject, and the illusion of having found an Archimedean standpoint, situated beyond historical and cultural contingency. They have long ceased to convince" (Benhabib, 1992: 4). In opposition to this she introduces her concept of interactive universalism, which I want to make use of in terms of what I am saying about the universally intended character of witnessing to the utopian.

> Interactive universalism acknowledges the plurality of modes of being human, and differences among humans, without endorsing all these pluralities and differences as morally and politically valid. While agreeing that normative disputes can be settled rationally, and that fairness, reciprocity and some procedure of universalizability are constituents, that is, necessary conditions of the moral standpoint, interactive universalism regards difference as a starting-point for reflection and action (Benhabib, 1992: 153).

Our embeddedness as subjects within a narrative framework is central to interactive universalism. As such we can reject the strong version of the so-called "Death of Man" thesis, which claims that "Man is forever caught in the web of fictive meaning, in chains of signification, in which the subject is merely another position in language" (Benhabib, 1992: 214). This thesis is incompatible with an interactive universalism for two reasons.

First, such a subject, unstructured by language or narrative, is incoherent. Our identities as subjects, whether individually or collectively, evolve in and through the stories we tell others and ourselves. Second, a subject unaffected by narrative structures and linguistic construals is a subject unable to be situated. These narratives play a fundamental role in the constitution of our identities. This extends the point made in Chapter Three, namely, that embeddedness and our embodiedness constitute our lives in general and the utopian as a way of being in the world more specifically. What the discussion here adds is that the utopian as universally intended not only emphasizes the particularity of instances that contribute to the utopian, but also retains a notion of normativity that is equally important to the critical impetus of any transformative thinking.

We can see how this notion of universal intent functions by considering the work of "integrative feminisms," which is described in the following way.

> [It is a] new universalism that will not deny the accumulated experience and knowledge of all past generations ...that ...will not accept the imposition of any monolithic, "universal" structures under which it is presumed all other people must be subsumed.... [It is a] new universalism that will challenge the universal mode, the logic of our development, science, technology, militarization, the nuclear option. A new universalism that will respect the plurality of different societies—of their philosophy, of their ideology, their traditions and cultures, one that will be rooted in the particular, one which will develop in the context of the dialectics of different civilizations, birthing a new cosmology (D'Souza, 1992: 141).[2]

Integrative feminisms not only seek to transform particular practices that affect women adversely, it is an emancipatory movement in the name of something like freedom for women that goes "beyond pressure for a single group and address[es] the whole of society" (Miles, 1996: xi).

Three things are worth noting here. First, there is a universal dimension to this work. Second, the idea that universalism is not simply an epistemological one, but also a political one that emerges from and responds to specific contexts. Third, there is a commitment to transforming universal structures, a point that I would add can be read in conjunction with my argument in Chapter Three that the structures of embodiment while universal are always already implicated in the lived experiences. The most significant point for my purposes is that integrative feminisms are motivated by "paradigms unashamedly informed by utopian goals," something witnessed to explicitly by the work of the National Black Women's Health Project "Women Hurt in Systems of Prostitution Engaged in Revolt" (WHISPER) (Miles, 1996: 142).

Founded in 1985 WHISPER is an organization of women who have survived degrading systems of prostitution and who are committed to ending this particular form of violence. It is comprised of women from diverse racial, ethnic, and economic backgrounds to create change in both personal and communal lives. To be sure, WHISPER is the acronym used to indicate a shared dehumanizing experience. However, instead of a shared experience that isolates them from others who have been excluded, the shared experience here links prostitutes together in ways that *open* them onto the world for transformation instead of a unity that absorbs their experiences into a single experience and consequently isolates them. Using the language of reversibility, let me explain this in the following way.

As utopian politics WHISPER, ontologically conditioned by reversibility and epistemologically guided by interactive universalism, is committed to the specific experiences of women with forms of dehumanization yet at the same time devoted to forms of liberation that transcend their particular locations. Second, WHISPER's aim is to make transformative links with other women's groups along with the wider public in hopes of bringing about societal transformation across different locations. Therefore, on a societal level WHISPER intends its practices to work for the freedom of those whose lives are affected in similar ways. What is important to see is that the sharing of the devastating effects of prostitution, instead of closing off those who undergo this particular affliction from others, is the basis from which transformative links are made. "In developing the particular voices of prostitutes," we are told, "they contribute to a general development of feminism as the inclusive, multi-centered movement it must be.... Increasingly, [however,] their outreach efforts include a global component" (Miles, 1996: 57). In short, WHISPER witnesses to the utopian demand that things be better by intending their thought and practices universally with the goal of freedom and societal transformation.

Let me summarize what I have said so far. Both the colloquial and technical understandings of testimony come together under the rubric of interpretation. Interpretation, then, is two-fold: we are interpreted by the utopian encounter, and we seek to make sense of this encounter both to ourselves and as it relates or extends to others. The witness to the utopian is to oneself, and a witness who testifies in thought and action to the universal dimensions of the utopian potential that has been unearthed. In this way, we begin to see how characteristics of what I want to call a "responsible witness" begin to emerge. What I want to do now is turn to this discussion and elaborate more fully these characteristics of what it means to be a responsible witness.

The question "What does it mean to be a responsible witness?" of course, could lead to a variety of responses. It could take the form of an answer something like "my moral duty to the utopian event is 'X'" where "X" means developing a notion of responsibility along the lines of, say, a Kantian approach where we try to get clear on what we mean by obligation to the utopian, and how this would apply to every situation where the question of responsible action is asked or assumed. It is not the first part of this that bothers me, but the last part. Such an approach, as I have suggested in various ways throughout, is not the kind of approach I want to take in thinking about the utopian. It may be interesting to think about the ideal abstract way of being responsible vis-à-vis the utopian (though I doubt that it is), but doing so will get us nowhere in actually living responsibly to the event that has interrupted us. In any regard, this kind of move is part and parcel to the utopian in its most traditional form, which I reject. In opposition to this, I want to say that responsibility is the attempt to act consistently in a way that remains faithful to the utopian event. The commitment is not to principles that are incontrovertible, but to principles that are held in the confidence that our action(s) on behalf of the utopian can be trusted to be a truthful response to the event that has radically disrupted our lives. In what follows, then, I want to argue for three characteristics of the responsible witness.

1. Fidelity to the encounter
2. Truthfulness of the content
3. Consistency in action

In the context of the discussion in the preceding sections, these are the minimal components that will be present in a responsible witness to the utopian. Let me begin with fidelity to the encounter.

To aid in developing this notion, I want to mention Simon Critchley's recent book, *Infinitely Demanding: Ethics of Commitment, Politics of Resistance* (Critchley, 2007). In this book, Critchley expresses not only a similar thought regarding grace as a utopian interruption that I argued in Chapter Two, he helpfully indicates the way that the event as a universal demand (similar to what I call universal intent) requires faithfulness to that event on our part. He writes:

> We begin with the experience of a demand or address, which is the event of grace, and the subject defines itself by approving of this event in a declaration of faith.... Subject and event come into being at the same time.... The subject defines itself by binding itself approvingly, in trothful truth, to the demand that the event makes upon it (Critchley 2007: 46; 47).

While Critchley (following Alain Badiou) speaks of faith here, I prefer to call this being a responsible witness. This passage suggests how the event addresses us, what I developed in Chapter Two as an advent. The connection with responsible testimony is that after a utopian disruption one binds themselves to that encounter. The characteristic of fidelity, then, is that of a commitment to the utopian moment, a commitment that involves the following. First, it is a commitment to an encounter that can and most likely will meet with great resistance, criticism and as such destroy the utopian impulse (or cover it over again). The commitment here is to the kernel of truth in the encounter that, despite changing conditions, will remain the same in its utopian demand. In this way, the commitment is to the promise of the utopian potential. As I will demonstrate in the following chapter, this is how one can read the criticisms of the South African Truth and Reconciliation Commission and its alternative to strict forms of deliberative democracy.

Second, the commitment is to the encounter itself. This is, following Gabriel Marcel, a new awareness between the I believe and the I exist that the utopian moment potentially opens, what Marcel calls creative fidelity. "My behavior," Marcel writes, "will be completely colored by this act embodying the decision that the commitment will not again be questioned (Marcel, 1964: 162). In effect, the commitment here is to oneself as a potentially new subject called forth in the utopian moment. This is where fidelity and interpretation, in the sense of self-interpretation, are linked in that by binding me to this event, the task of self-understanding is now different.

Third, the fidelity to the encounter is the commitment to the way this moment has the potential to transform everyone. That is, the commitment here is to the universally intended dimension of the event, which is to say that even though situations will change, the commitment to the encounter is to the emancipatory kernel that is universally applicable. In the end, commitment to the utopian requires us to pledge ourselves to that encounter as both new subjects who have undergone the moment, and to others who though are situated differently than we are, nevertheless (we claim) fall under the potential of the utopian to transform them as well. This point raises the issue of how we, as responsible witnesses faithful to the utopian encounter, engage the world on behalf of the utopian. With the idea of commitment as that which opens the question of engagement in mind, I would like to suggest two ways of understanding the question of engagement on behalf of the utopian. The first proposal is again offered by Simon Critchley, and the second by Gianni Vattimo.

To orient Critchley's understanding, we can understand engagement first, as emerging from the order of reversibility as the condition for being-together and remaining-apart. If this is the case, engagement takes place in-between or following Critchley, interstitially (See Critchley, 2007: Ch. 4). Reversibility, recall, signifies the ontological gap that, when linked with the utopian, reminds us how the utopian, grounded in the lived bodily experiences of individuals is not a solipsistic occurrence, but rather intertwines us with those that are separate from us. However, the ontological gap of reversibility demands a response that can only take place in-between, an in-between that is the space of reversibility. One way to understand this is again to invoke Marcel (1964) and say that the engagement that occurs as creative fidelity can be understood as an engagement in between too much adherence to one position (e.g., a certain theory of justice), and too little adherence to anything (e.g., viewing engagement as an endless play of irony or differences). In this way, engagement as in-between is creative in the way that Mark Taylor writing in a different context suggests. He writes:

> Even when expected, emergence is surprising—without surprise, there is no novelty; without novelty, there is no creativity; without creativity there is no life. To live within the confines of the expected, which seems to provide stability, security, and certainty, is to be dead even when alive; to be exposed to the unexpected is to be open to the chance of life—and death.... Restlessness need not always lead to the melancholy of unhappy unconsciousness that wallows in interminable mourning but can engender the vitality that in-forms creativity (Taylor, 2007: 345).

Learning to live (ethically and politically) in this gap, in the space of reversibility is the work of becoming faithful, the work of being a responsible witness. This is why I agree with Critchley when he concludes the following.

> [This fidelity to the event] permits ethics to be approached as a subjective process, or better perhaps, a process of the formation of ethical subjectivity, where a self commits itself with fidelity to a concrete situation, a singular occurrence that places a demand on the self. Yet, this emphasis on the singular and the concrete does not entail relativism, but rather situated universalism where an event can only be justified if it is addressed to all. My commitment to the situation motivates ethical action whose justification exceeds the situation and works to bring about its transformation and amelioration (Critchley, 2007: 49).

Situated or interactive universalism guides our faithful action and allows this action to be truthful to the event itself (I will return to this below).

There is another way to think of how we might engage the world, especially in light of the conflict of interpretations that will undoubtedly challenge our on-going interpretation of the utopian. This is a response based on the work of Gianni Vattimo.

As an introductory remark, it is worth noting that Vattimo himself has weighed in on the need for the utopian claiming that we should perhaps keep talking about the practical importance of the utopian because "the term is evocative to one degree or another, of the 'emancipation project.'"(Vattimo, 2006: 20). Yet he also points out that if the utopian is to be effective for our contemporary setting, then it must be conceptually "re-expressed in a new form, with characteristics more in conformity with our post-metaphysical era" (Vattimo, 2006: 18). In general, he offers both a practical and conceptual challenge to reconsider the utopian that is at once post-metaphysical in its understanding and still able to guide the engaged work of concrete emancipation. In particular, Vattimo's thought helps us to think about how, as responsible witnesses, we engage others and remain faithful to the event.

To be sure, even though Vattimo's proposal, like Critchley's, offers guidance to our lived existence with the many conflicts of interpretation, he does not propose a "how to" manual that explains the *a priori* procedures for installing his now familiar version of weak thought into our daily lives so that agreement or resolution in these matters will be guaranteed. On the contrary, Vattimo's understanding of hermeneutics, while to be sure not unsympathetic to the place of proceduralism (see, for instance his chapter on proceduralism in *Nihilism and Emancipation*), suspends such questions in favor of engaging each other without a preconceived notion of unity before engagement or an assumption that the engagement will yield some kind of unity in the end. As such, Vattimo, like Nietzsche, Kierkegaard, Heidegger and others before him, places the responsibility of witnessing to what he calls "weak thought" solely on us instead of the procedures that, in the name of ethics, tempt us (to use a Kierkegaardian turn of phrase) to trust in them (in the name of reason and responsibility), only to remove us from taking responsibility—all, ironically, in the name of "being responsible." In this way, Vattimo's "weak thought," at least in this regard, is a resource for taking up the question "How do we engage the world on behalf of the utopian?"

The idea of "weak thought" is best understood as his response to learning to live "after metaphysics." To speak of "after" metaphysics is, according to Vattimo, to get beyond the existence of metaphysics, or better the persistence of metaphysical thinking that is presupposed in our moral and political practices of which the utopian is paradigmatic. If we accept Vattimo's and others critique of metaphysics we also accept the critique of a conventional view of the utopian understood in the following way.

First, there is a belief that the world possesses a certain fixed structure that can be discovered and reflected in our practices (utopian or otherwise). Whether this is described in terms of "Cartesian certainty," "Transcendental structure," or an "Archimedean point," the same assumption runs through them: there is something out there, independent of our minds that can be discovered, and once discovered can enable us to align our (utopian) visions of the world with the way the world "really is." And this phrase "really is" is important, because its very locution betrays the metaphysical worldview from both sides of the same conceptual fence, namely, that there is a real structure to the world that, once deduced, can insure the veracity of our visions of the world, thus making such a vision the vision to which everyone should adhere.[3] And while such language is often associated with totalitarian regimes, fundamentalisms of all stripes or fanatics, this view is, if we follow Vattimo's line of thinking here, conceptually the same even in the more tolerant, inclusive and progressive views (while, to be sure, practically different). Both views, when presented not so much as the way the world should be but instead the way the world is (best), rely on a metaphysical view that is ultimately the same and one that Vattimo believes we are better off not having.

Second, Vattimo's project of thinking "after metaphysics" affirms and extends the Nietzschean announcement that "God is dead, and we have killed him," a pronouncement that opens the possibility of becoming nihilistic enough (and the project Vattimo has taken up). Like Nietzsche, Vattimo does not intend this as a metaphysical claim, knowing that to make such a claim is to presuppose a metaphysical stance similar to those making such claims on behalf the existence of the world as it "really" is. Instead, such a claim announces a new era, a new opening that Vattimo characterizes as "postmodern " insofar as it "is the epoch in which reality can no longer be conceived of as a structure solidly tied to a sole foundation that philosophy would have the task of knowing, or perhaps that religion would have the task of adoring" (Vattimo, 2002: 5). What this means, then, is that in order to avoid the potential violence of metaphysics, even in its more tolerant forms, we should proceed differently, along the lines of what Vattimo calls "weak thought."

Weak thought, above all, affirms the rejection of old-style metaphysics, and proceeds according to the Nietzschean principle that "everything is an interpretation, and that's an interpretation too," and for my purposes extends to the utopian in this way. Adopting this Nietzschean claim not only allows us to think of the utopian as one claim among the conflict of interpretations, but in the light of the opening that after metaphysics provides, it makes possible once more the narratives of the utopian that call to us, move us and transform us toward making the world better. In the light of this Nietzschean hermeneutical principle, coupled with the critique of metaphysics, there are two important points that factor into reconfiguring the utopian as post-metaphysical, a notion that fits with what I said above regarding universal intent.

First, we can again make a case and offer an interpretation with confidence about our understanding of the utopian. And this confidence is allowed because we have given up on the view that there is, should or might be a utopian vision that reflects the way the world is in its claims that this vision is what should be the case, where the should in old-school metaphysics is linked to a "more real" version of the world. Second, and a result of giving up on the utopian as a working out of some transcendental structure, we are to offer our visions of the utopian with humility. After all, if we take the Nietzschean claim that "everything is an interpretation, and that's an interpretation too" as our guide, then the utopian claims made on us, and we make on others are just that: claims. And as claims they enjoy no special status vis-à-vis the way the world is in itself, but instead demand we give an account of them (not giving up on reason itself), and witness to the transformative power of the utopian. In this regard, the utopian is just speculation, but speculation that matters to practical life.

Does this, in the end, mean that Vattimo has no principles? There is a principle that seems to guide him throughout his work, which is that the only right is the right to be heard, which is another way of reminding us of the work of witnessing to the utopian. It is in Vattimo's notion of becoming "nihilistic enough," that allows us to see the workings of reversibility in the previous chapter, and now in what I have been arguing here the work of testimony. In short, we become converted.

I mean by this, first, our willingness to enter the world of those with whom we are in conflict. As we saw in Chapter Four, this is not a Kantian imaginative leap hailed by the likes of Hannah Arendt and others (as helpful as this is), nor, I will add here, is it in line with hermeneutics traditionally conceived. Fundamentally, it is a willingness to suspend our own frameworks in favor of those with whom we seek engagement, and with whom we are in conflict. I say "suspend" intentionally, because in becoming converted I am not suggesting that we destroy what makes our position our own. I am borrowing a line of thought from Kierkegaard and suggesting that in order to respond, we must interrupt our own needs to "understand," "make sense of," or "get clear on" that with which we are in conflict, needs usually revealed in the attempts to put procedural rules around such engagement. Nor am I suggesting that in some fit of warm, fuzzy essentialism that we, in the name of celebrating difference for the sake of difference, attempt to walk away saying "well, we are on the same page, with a few slight, unimportant differences." I am talking about being converted to the very things that establish the difference, things that matter most to our identities—for instance, like one's understanding of the world based on religious commitments. This does not mean, to be very clear, that in being converted we accept as our own the other's views themselves, where the logic of conversion is converted from one to another. Conversion, therefore, is neither an imaginative leap to what Hume called "fellow-feeling," nor is it conversion as acceptance. Conversion is, following Kierkegaard, suspension much along the lines that Abraham did with the ethical in his willingness to sacrifice Isaac, something that, if this story is helpful in any way, demands a one-to-one relationship that looks like a parasite on the back of conditional ethical and political demands (Kierkegaard, 1983).[4]

Conversion is, furthermore, different from how traditional hermeneutics might understand it. In this regard, Vattimo's hermeneutics is different from more conventional versions. Traditionally, whether under the guise of seeking understanding along the lines of the Gadamerian "fusion of horizons," the often explicit goal of hermeneutics as a philosophy of dialogue is to make that which is unfamiliar familiar through dialogical encounters. Vattimo's "post-metaphysical" Nietzschean-Heideggerian hermeneutics jettisons this notion, I suggest, in favor of a letting be of the position that threatens us. This "letting be," however, is not a refusal to engage critically, which goes to the point I have been making in this section. To the contrary, with the disappearance of any ultimate foundation to which we appeal, the capability of saying "this is wrong" is still allowed, but only insofar as such claims are to be argued for (retaining reason), and put forth with the awareness that without the ultimate foundation, our critical responses are just that: responses that possess no special relation with the way things "really are" as in old-style metaphysics. A good illustration of how I am using conversion can be seen in the recent German film *Das Leben der Anderen* (The Lives of Others).

The movie revolves around the monitoring practices of the East Berlin's Stasi or secret police in the 1980s. Stasi agent Gerd Wiesler, an adamant supporter of the communist regime, is hired to monitor, through listening and watching, the lives of the playwright Georg Dreyman and his lover, Christa-Maria Sieland, both of whom are suspected to be Western sympathizers. Through a series of encounters Wiesler comes to see that even though Dreyman does have Western sympathies, Wiesler becomes converted to the plight of both Dreyman and Sieland. In the end, Wiesler places himself at risk to destroy evidence that would, if found, bring severe consequences for Dreyman's activities. Wiesler, then, is found by his superiors to have failed in his task and demoted significantly. What is important in this movie, as I have very briefly described it here, is that in order for Wiesler to act in the way he does, he becomes converted not to Western ways of living, but to the lives of Dreyman and Sieland, which, with Wiesler's listening and attention, now demands something of Wiesler that was not possible before his conversion though attention to their lives. In short, Wiesler suspends his own position, allowing him to adopt the lives of those he is charged to destroy, while he remains committed to his own position in the Stasi. To emphasize, Wiesler's suspension of his position does not mean he stops being a faithful servant of the Stasi or the East Berlin government. He remains, after he is converted to Dreyman and Sieland, presumably committed to its ideals, and still works for the government (though admittedly in a less important role). In this regard, Wiesler, I suggest, illustrates the kind of conversion I am linking with Vattimo's charge to become nihilistic enough.

Such a proposition, however, is not so easily adopted for at least two reasons. First, there is the sense that in becoming converted in the way I am suggesting we give away our selves and become at the mercy of those we seek to understand. I have suggested, despite this, that conversion as becoming nihilistic enough does not mean a giving away *in toto* of that which shapes us fundamentally, but means suspending it in the service of engagement. Second, such a position is often made untenable because of the temptation of proceduralism that, we believe, insures agreement, resolution of fundamental differences, and guarantees unity. In other words, even if we agree with Vattimo that we are bound by our own historicity, and this affects us and is affected as we become converted by paying attention to this as we cultivate an ethic of listening, this does not make it any easier in trying to suspend the desire for guaranteeing communication on the way to agreement. Let me offer a different illustration from the 2008 campaign for president in the United States, an issue that has plagued now President Obama. This example in particular raises the issue of engagement with conflicting interpretations.

Both Hilary Clinton and Barack Obama were asked (Web, CNN, July 23, 2007) "Would you be willing to meet separately during the first year of your administration, with leaders of Syria, Iran, Venezuela and others to bridge the gap between our countries?" In response to this question Obama said he would, stating that "The notion that somehow not talking to countries is punishment to them — which has been the guiding diplomatic principle of this [Bush] administration — is ridiculous." In contrast to this, Clinton was hesitant to make such a promise. While agreeing to pursue diplomatic efforts, she concluded that "you don't promise a meeting until you know the intentions. I don't want to be used for propaganda purposes and don't want to make a situation worse." Though I am certain there is much more to their respective positions than a sound bite communicates, still their responses illustrate points I am making.

First, Obama's initial remark, which he later tempered after resounding criticism, seems to reflect a hermeneutical orientation closer to Vattimo's insofar as it appears to be guided by the principle that everyone deserves a right to be heard. Obama's promise to engage these radically different, and even threatening positions, reflects a primacy of listening and attentiveness in the service of engagement. Clinton's response, it seems, reflects more of a communicative ethics position, which is to say, she privileges the clarity of conditions beforehand in the service of engagement. One position values that which is different and risks opening up lines of communication with those positions that are in conflict, while the other position, even though undoubtedly not denying difference, represents a more proceduralist understanding of engaging the conflict of interpretations. To bring this back to Vattimo, his ethic of listening that emerges from embracing our shared creation of nihilism stands between those, on the one hand, who are often viewed as sacrificing truth and communication at the cost of affirming difference (such as the way some read Richard Rorty), and those, on the other hand, that are often viewed as sacrificing difference for communicative truth (such as the way some read Habermas and to a lesser extent Gadamer).

Let me summarize this section. First, a nihilistic hermeneutics enables us to engage that with which we are in conflict in ways that require more attention and listening than either a position that celebrates difference at the expense of critical judgment, or forms of proceduralism that highlight agreement and unity at the expense of communication and difference that matters in terms of issues in the public sphere. Second, the ethic of listening shifts the question from "How do I understand that which is different," a tenet of hermeneutics both in its classical and some contemporary versions, to the question, in the light of listening as risking or being converted in the sense I have been speaking, to "What does the other and this situation (who may even seek to destroy me) demand?" At the risk of repetition, let me stress that even though we allow the question to be shifted, this does not mean critical engagement is prevented and a hyper-relativistic flourishing of many perspectives is adopted. Becoming converted, in addition to becoming more perspectival through deepened attentiveness, allows critical moments to emerge on their own (if in fact they do) and tempts our need to demand of such moments *a priori* procedural guarantees, or, our demand that difference be accepted for the sake of difference alone. Both positions, besides suffering from the same kind of metaphysical hangover that Vattimo calls into question, often cut short the very engagement initially sought.

What, then, is demanded of us beyond the willingness to be converted? I would like to suggest that in addition to becoming converted, a way we can live our nihilism more faithfully to the demands placed on us of witnessing to the utopian, rather than the demands we place on engagement, is to become bilingual, a bilingualism that as a result of this shared nihilism for which we are co-responsible presupposes the conflict of interpretations.

Becoming bilingual, or perhaps multilingual, may appear easier than becoming converted, but along with the need to be converted, becoming bilingual is a way of understanding how the call of nihilism presses against us the question of responsible engagement. Becoming bilingual, foremost, does not mean simply learning the native language of those with whom we are in conflict (as helpful as this might be in public discourse). It means, instead, learning the language that shapes one's being in the world (to follow both Gadamer and Heidegger). In learning such language, we learn to listen more attentively to how the demands of those with whom we are in conflict shape them the way our own language, which I intentionally use broadly here, shapes the very way we engage them in these conflicting contexts. In other words, becoming bilingual is not asking everyone to speak the language of North American democracy no matter how much we good North Americans believe in it (whether religious or secular). Neither is it, if we follow Vattimo along the lines I suggest above, learning their language in order to show them the ways they are un-reasonable and/or ir-rational. It is, rather, a part of the process of learning how to suspend our own framework with its attending modern needs, which is most often understood as making that which is unfamiliar familiar (again, even if this is done under the sign of tolerance, human rights and other attempts to understand the other better). Becoming bilingual means learning how to speak, when to speak, in what ways, under what conditions, to whom, and under what kind of circumstances. In this way, practicing bilingualism is an ad hoc enterprise that requires a disciplined attentiveness on our part. As such, becoming bilingual is analogous to Aristotle's *phronemon* in his *Nichomachean Ethics* who knows what to think, what to feel, in what way and for what ends. And like the *phronemon* the one who becomes bilingual knows this is a disciplined task that, instead of yielding principles that we invoke to do the work for us, requires of us a disciplined way of comporting ourselves—an *ethos* in the Greek sense, as a way of behaving toward each other where the question of what constitutes the good life is contested. Let me offer a personal illustration.

In my university, a strongly Lutheran identified university that is equally humanistic in its orientation, there is no shortage of fundamentalist students who believe, for instance, that the first eleven chapters of Genesis are historically accurate, that they can find God's will through such a reading of scripture, and that "What Would Jesus Do?" is a much better educational philosophy than anything derived from a Lutheran understanding of higher education. And to be sure, such students plague many faculty for these beliefs. But these students never surprise me (perhaps having grown up in the South as a Southern Baptist helps in this regard). I am, however, almost always astonished at my colleagues' responses (most of whom mean well), colleagues who are amazed that students could in any way hold to such beliefs in the light of universal reason that through a good dose of self-doubt can free them from their self-incurred tutelage (yes, my colleagues are at once Cartesian and Kantian). My surprise is twofold.

First, there is the confidence (over confidence?) in the power of reason to set such students free, a power pursued under the umbrella of "more education" and more exposure, in most regards, to the canon of Enlightenment evangelists. These positions, it seems to me, refuse to accept the notion that students simply do not believe, like they do, in the Enlightenment project, do not believe that there is such a thing as "universal Man," and instead believe that if we are to get along it will be when all bow at the feet of Jesus and not the eighteenth-century understanding of right reason. Second, and more surprising to me is the equally persistent refusal on the part of some of my colleagues to learn the language of these fundamentalist students in a way that is not to be used this against them (which is not the same as learning to engage them critically), but instead, as I suggested above, in a way that attempts to learn the language that shapes their being in the world. In this way, my colleagues refuse to become converted through refusing to become bilingual, both ways I am suggesting, following Vattimo, that we learn to live our nihilism as a means to engage responsible in the interpretive and adjudicatory process with the conflict of interpretations.

To be sure, I am not naïve enough to believe that doing what I am suggesting would, on even a rudimentary level, guarantee that such students would ever stop being fundamentalist. I am suggesting, instead, that becoming bilingual in this way can help us to turn the question from "Why would you believe that?" to "What is demanded of me in this situation?"—A situation I now know, after taking on board the ways my interlocutor is shaped, I know in a more "thick" way? This latter question, to be certain, is one of understanding, but understanding as a demand to be heard, instead of a notion of understanding that demands you make your unfamiliar self a part of my familiar framework, which of course for many of us is the same as saying that the unfamiliar must make themselves familiar to all so that their position "makes sense," where making sense is really most likely some stereotypically Hegelian dream of knowing everything. Over against this is the option, following Vattimo, to live our nihilism, which what I have been saying about becoming a responsible witness to the utopian, poses a risk that carries with it a notion of responsibility that becomes most apparent when, to use a turn of phrase from Wittgenstein, criteria or procedures fail us, and do so devastatingly.

Here we can return to what I mentioned briefly above. The gap that reversibility opens is a gap where failure looms, and in a space where we must be willing to go to reveal the hidden potential of the utopian. In doing so, we are, dare I say, engaging in a more authentic mode of witnessing, even if the authenticity here is first and foremost failure, which would make this kind of responsible witnessing an "inauthentic authenticity." It is in this space of failure that Vattimo's project, and the way I am extending it, can be of service in the conflict with commitments, a conflict that demands more than the adherence of procedures that, in their best efforts, fail and leave us with the question of "living ethically" together. It is, finally, if we are to take Vattimo seriously as I think we should, learning to live the shared vocation of the utopian as nihilism. In the end, both Critchley and Vattimo offer proposals as to how we engage the world and both suggest that engagement with the world requires one to be truthful. In this light, I want to claim that truthfulness is the second general characteristic of being a responsible witness to the utopian, following fidelity as the first.

First, following what we saw earlier, to suggest that something is universally intended and applicable to all is to suggest that the utopian reflects something beyond our own subjective belief. It also reflects an awareness beyond the mere subjective beliefs of either others or us. It is, we might say, a confidence in that which is beyond the mere subjective and that to which the emancipatory element points. In the end, to speak of being truthful for me is to speak about the practice of the one witnessing to the encounter in particular ways. To extend this, I would like to employ the distinction made by Bernard Williams between sincerity and accuracy. Williams tells us that sincerity "merely implies that people say what they believe to be true—that is, what they believe. Accuracy implies care, reliability, and so on, in discovering and coming to believe the truth (Williams, 2005: 154).[5] How do these relate to being responsible? Responsible sincerity is saying what we believe, which is to say that in our witness to the truthfulness of the utopian we are constructing, with other people, the truth of our account. Here sincerity and creative fidelity go hand-in-hand insofar as we become a certain reflection of that which we profess, and that which is then returned to us through the encounter (via reversibility) with others. We can, then, agree with Williams when he writes:

> In the social or political case, where the presence of other people is vital, sincerity helps to construct or create truth. Drawn to bind myself to the other's shared values, to make my own beliefs and feelings steadier (to make them, at the limit, for the first time into beliefs), I become what with increasing steadiness I can sincerely profess; I become what I have sincerely declared to

them, or perhaps I become my interpretation of their interpretation I what I have sincerely declared to them (Williams, 2002:
203–204).

The construction of the truthfulness of the account of the utopian encounter relies on a way of orienting oneself not only to the
event, but also to the practice of witnessing to the event, a responsible
practice of being sincere in this regard. With sincerity, then, there is
also accuracy.

If sincerity is more about saying what we believe in a way that constitutes us and others to the event, accuracy is about establishing this
belief. Accuracy, I want to suggest is less about the persistency of the
content of the utopian as matching up with some metaphysical way the
world really is, and more about how, in light of the utopian, we orient
ourselves to the lived experience of the world that we now want to accurately extend from the utopian moment. Accuracy, I would offer further, is establishing the correctness of our belief, but doing so in a way
that is more realistic with the situations that demand a witness of the
utopian. The realism here is an awareness that the truthfulness of our
content is neither waiting for us to discover it, nor is it pre-established
beforehand. Instead, accuracy is a way of recognizing that political life
is full of uncertainty and not some fantasy that projects the possibility of something disconnected from our lived existence. Accuracy, as
a way of establishing the sincerity of our beliefs, is a practice of learning to assess both our own perspective and those of others in the light
of and service to the utopian demand. Accuracy in this regard is the
awareness that on behalf of the utopian we witness in institutions and
situations at particular given times, and responsible testimony is to the
way these situations actually are, rather some idealized way they might
be in some disconnected, abstract sense. In this light, sincerity and accuracy as characteristics of truthfulness reflect how a responsible witness will practice consistency in action, which is the final element of
being a responsible witness.

First, consistency in action cannot *a priori* be determined ahead
of time. Contra ethical theories that insist delimiting before the

fact the proper characteristics of criteria like duty or responsibility, consistency in action is always determined by the specifics of the situation. In this way, a responsible witness is always attentive to the conditions in which one is called to act, and sincerity and accuracy emerge from this awareness. As I have said, however, this does not preclude making universally intended claims, but instead recognizes that these are particular claims not abstracted from the situation itself. What begins as a particular lived bodily event of the utopian demand that things be different becomes, if it is to transcend the parochial confines of one's subjective experience, a universally intended possibility for human transformation. Among other things, this is the lesson of Sojourner Truth, King and in this chapter integrative feminisms, all of which intend freedom not simply as a conceptual potential but a practical one that our lives witness to in action.

Second, consistency in action, if it cannot be determined ahead of time, is based on a wager and risk that how we act in a way that takes care of the utopian is done so without the assurance that it might be the correct response. Ricoeur puts this best when, discussing similar issues, he writes that "We wager on a certain set of values and then try to be consistent with them; verification is therefore a question of our whole life. No one escapes this" (Ricoeur, 1986: 312). Following Ricoeur, we can say that there is no causal connection between the manner in which we respond and whether or not that action is true in the sense of "True" for all and eternity. If I am correct on the first point that we cannot know ahead of time how to respond responsibly, then it will make extremely difficult (if not impossible) the attempt to calculate the maximal benefit and minimal risk in a particular situation so that we know what we are doing is consistent with regard to the utopian demand. None of this will preclude any of what I have said about being truthful. Truthfulness is a way of practicing the universally intended claim that not all positions are equally viable in a way that opens to ourselves and others the liberative potential of the utopian. Consistency in action will reflect the particular truth that is, as an emancipatory truth, the truth of all. Let me offer the following example from popular culture to extend this point.

I am a fan of Johnny Cash's music. His music carries certain elements of the utopian as I have been developing it throughout, and demonstrates the way I see fidelity, truthfulness, and consistency in action as characteristics of a responsible witness. In particular, Cash's awareness of political responsibility to the utopian demand that things be different can be summed up in the phrase "no one is free until all are free." Such songs like "All God's Children Ain't Free," along with others over the course of his career, suggest the following.

First, pursuing freedom means we engage the world in a way that promotes an idea of what it means to be "a free human being." This image, as his songs about both literal and metaphorical prisons reveal, is one where people are treated with dignity and respect and an image that challenges the notion that humans are simply means to the ends of society. In this light, his song like "The Ballad of Ira Hayes," embodies the kind of utopian potential that I have been arguing for, in particular the element of interruption. Second, however, it means recognizing that not all possess the freedom they should have. This echoes the point I made in Chapter Three that there are structures of embodiment that we all possess, but because of lived bodily experience these structures are often incapable of being enacted. Finally, Cash's call for the "freedom for all" entails the responsibility to work for freedom that while in theory might be available to all, is not practically possessed by them. In a song like, "Man in Black," then, we get a glimpse of this awareness and the responsibility it entails when he sings of how wearing black symbolizes not only the solidarity with those for whom freedom is not yet a realized potential, but the need to work toward such enactment in the lives of those who otherwise have little or no hope.

In what might be an odd combination, Cash's emphasis on freedom expresses an attitude close to Jean-Paul Sartre, who famously in "Existentialism as a Humanism" writes something similar.

When I declare that freedom in every concrete circumstance can have no other aim than to want itself, if man has once become aware that in his forlornness he imposes values, he can no longer want but one thing, and that is freedom, as the basis of all values.... We want freedom for freedom's sake and in every particular circumstance. And in wanting freedom we discover that it depends entirely on the freedom of others, and that the freedom of others depends on ours. Of course, freedom as the definition of man does not depend on others, but as soon as there is involvement, I am obliged to want others to have freedom at the same time that I want my own freedom. I can take freedom as my goal only if I take that of others as the goal as well (Guignon and Derk Pereboom, 2001: 306.)

Even though this is the language of existentialism, it shares with Cash's view that "no one is free until all are free," which is a sentiment that reveals the on-going notion of witnessing to the witness of the utopian on behalf of those who are incapable of living the potential of the utopian itself. Further, Sartre states rather explicitly what Cash does implicitly, namely, the idea that even though humans by being born humans are free (the ontological notion of freedom), this does not mean that all humans possess concrete freedom(s) (political freedom). Finally, this detour through Cash and Sartre helps us to see that responsibility is about how we engage the world with awareness that, once arrested by the claims of the utopian, we have the task to work for and secure the possibilities revealed by the utopian that many if not most lack. Only then can the utopian demand that things be different engage in the responsible practice of "creative fidelity."

To conclude this chapter, I want to offer three summary points. First, to speak on behalf of the utopian is to give testimony to its interruptive power that potentially transforms not just us, but everyone. This universal intent is the emancipatory "what-if" hidden but now revealed in the utopian. Moreover, this need to witness opens the question of engagement with the world on behalf of the utopian, and demands a realistic awareness of the conflict of interpretations that undoubtedly will refuse the utopian, yet still calls those who have witnessed the utopian and now are witnesses to it to hold fast to its advent. To witness in this fashion, I have argued, is to do so in a responsible way. In particular, responsible witnesses are bound to the encounter, engage the world in truthful practice, and act on behalf of the utopian in a consistent manner. Together the task of the witness who gives testimony to the utopian is disciplined. The question that I want to ask now that I have offered the final element of the utopian is this: "Does the utopian as I have developed it exist in any political event?" To be sure, throughout I have indicated several concrete examples for each element. What I propose to do in the final chapter is offer an extended discussion of a political movement that, in my estimation, engages in utopian politics of the kind I have offered, bringing together all of the elements of the utopian.

Chapter Six

The Utopian Function of Forgiveness

In this final Chapter I want to discuss the South African Truth and Reconciliation Commission (TRC) as a political movement that instantiates the elements of the utopian in the ways I have argued in the previous chapters. The general thesis of this chapter is the TRC is utopian in a non-conventional sense. The more particular claims are as follows. First, the TRC, with the centrality of forgiveness to its political efforts, introduces an alternative to how we might imagine living together in just ways. As such, the TRC interrupts more traditional notions of justice. Second, the TRC's option relies on the other elements of the utopian that I have developed, those of embodiment/embodiedness, reversibility and, finally, being a witness to the utopian interruption. In this way, third, we can see not only how the utopian work of the TRC challenges our settled notions of justice, but also how it is subsequently criticized by, those who believe the TRC is misguided. It is precisely at this point the utopian politics of the TRC engages the work of deliberative democracy. My aim, therefore, is to show how the TRC is utopian, but also how a proponent of this utopian work might respond to advocates of deliberative democracy.

To be sure, even though it can be said to reflect more conventional elements of the utopian I discussed in Chapter One, it is important to emphasize that this is *not* the reason we should embrace the TRC as a politics of utopian potential. Instead, we should embrace it because it reflects elements of a non-conventional understanding of the utopian in the following ways. First, the TRC is located at a specific point in time. In this way, it does not exist in some extra-historical manner, or in an objective way that relies on an abstract notion of justice. Second, and related, the TRC at its utopian best, (despite how some may either read its work, or what proponents of its work may claim), is not about a potential state (perfected or otherwise) that, with the proper work, can be actualized. One need only consider its many flaws to respond to this. Rather, the work of the TRC, with all of its flaws and its questionable practices (like granting amnesty), is still worthy of the label "utopian" but in the way that is non-conventional. To develop my claims, I first want to utilize the following story as my framework.

Amy Biehl was murdered in the Gugulethu Township, in Cape Town on August 25, 1993. She was on a Fulbright Scholarship and was affiliated with the Community Law Center at the University of the Western Cape where she was pursuing her studies for a Ph.D. in Political Science. On the afternoon of her death, she was on her way to drop off three of her colleagues in Gugulethu, when her vehicle came under attack by people who were running towards it and throwing stones. The stones smashed the windscreen and windows of the car. One of the stones hit Amy Biehl on her head, causing her to bleed profusely. She could not continue driving so she got out of her car and ran towards a garage across the road. However, her attackers pursued her relentlessly and continued to throw stones at her. One of the perpetrators tripped her and caused her to fall. Surrounded by approximately ten people she was continually stoned and finally stabbed. She died as a result of the injuries inflicted on her.

The assailants, who admitted both to the stoning and stabbing, applied for amnesty under the TRC. They were eventually given amnesty with Amy Biehl's parents granting approval. Amy's parents went to South Africa, met with the victims and the parents of the victims, and, in the spirit of their daughter's work, approved of the amnesty request. In a word, Amy Biehl's parents, by their actions, testified both to the work of their daughter and to the transformative power of the TRC. As a result, we are told, the Biehls have continued Amy's work in South Africa establishing community services, educational opportunities, and other services so that the work of healing and reconciliation can continue. This response, on the part of the Biehls, demonstrates the centrality of the notion of forgiveness in the political work of the TRC. Before I turn to a more detailed discussion of the utopian function of forgiveness as the key to understanding the utopian politics of the TRC, I want to indicate, more generally, how the work of the Biehls, in the aftermath of their daughter's death, illustrates the elements of the utopian in previous chapters.

The first thing to note is that the transformative work that the Biehls engage in arises in the wake of an interruptive event, the death of Amy. The interruption here is one that is tragic in the most extreme sense. As I have intimated with other examples, the utopian demand that things be different often emerges from an experience of degradation (Sojourner Truth and WHISPER), or violence and death as in the case of Amy. Put differently, second, the utopian is located not in some external space that calls us, or is that toward which we are moving to actualize it. Rather, the utopian demand is unearthed in the material conditions of both embodiment and lived bodily experiences. In this way, the example of Amy Biehl (and the politics of forgiveness sought by the TRC) illustrates in a different way what we saw with Sojourner Truth, namely, that the utopian is always tied to the lived bodily conditions that bring about the demand that things be different. Third, the language used by the Biehls to describe the relationship with the community and their daughter's killers can, I submit, be best viewed as the language of reversibility. In a recent interview her parents describe their relationship with Amy as one of "becoming her." One way to interpret this claim is that they have reversed positions with her, even in death, and this reversibility has enabled them to return to the community where she was murdered. In addition, their ability to work in this community that created her killers is due to their ability to "come to terms" or "understand" the situation in which Amy worked and was killed. There is reversibility on the part of Amy and the community (before her death), the Biehls with Amy (before but especially after her death), and the Biehls with the community in which their only commonality is the death of their daughter. In this particular case, the ontological condition of reversibility creates the possibility of transformation on many levels (Biehl, 1999).[1]

Fourth, the Biehls reflect the notion of responsible witness discussed in the last chapter. Let me elaborate this. The interruptive moment brings a demand on two fronts. On the one hand, it is a demand to be interpreted, i.e., attempt to understand the event itself.

On the other hand, it is an interruptive demand that, as the Biehls attest, interprets them, which is to say demands of them something new. In and through this incredibly tragic and violent event, the utopian potential, in the work of the Biehls, is disclosed. As such, they exemplify the work of testimony.

In particular, they describe their work as a "carrying on," or a "witnessing to," this encounter of the death of their daughter which, in turn furthers the work of the TRC and its aims at disrupting and potentially transforming our deeply held beliefs in retributive justice. Though her parents did not directly hear the specific accounts of the TRC prior to her death (i.e., the mechanics by which the TRC works), after her death they became aware of the liberative efforts of the TRC (and Amy's participation in this work). In their words, only by coming to an "understanding" whereby they could empathize with the families of the perpetrators, could they fully carry on Amy's work—and by extension the TRC. As a result of their coming to terms with Amy's work and the work of the TRC, in addition to coming to terms with the devastating effects of apartheid, the Biehls witnessed to the work of the TRC. More significantly, they witnessed to, i.e. carried on, the transformative affect of *forgiveness* by remaining committed to the transformation of the environment that created their daughter's killers. It is here, then, that we can ask the question that I want to take up below: What, in the work of the TRC, is the utopian function of forgiveness?

The TRC offers a politics of forgiveness that responds differently to events that cry out for retribution. It seeks to release those who have been victims (including victimizers) of apartheid's destructive powers so that the future of both individuals and communities can be opened to new possibilities for existing together. In this manner, the TRC is universalistic in its intent and situated in its practice. What is often not clear is the way that the TRC, in its many elements, understands forgiveness. Even though there is a commitment to forgiveness as a potentially new way forward, forgiveness itself receives little sustained treatment. In what follows, therefore, I want to offer a way of understanding not just the notion of forgiveness that is at work in the

TRC, but the notion of forgiveness that exemplifies the utopian in the way I have been developing it.

The thinker that helps best in this task is Hannah Arendt. Arendt, arguably more than any other philosopher, gives special place to forgiveness in ethical and political action. According to her, forgiveness provides release to "the web of human relations," which is to say that whether we trespass against the other or the other trespasses against us, we trespass and are trespassed against in a web of relations that constantly needs chances to begin again. She writes:

> [Our web of relations] ...needs forgiving, dismissing, in order to make it possible for life to go on by constantly releasing men from what they have done unknowingly. Only through this constant mutual release from what they do can men remain free agents, only by constant willingness to change their minds and start again can they be trusted with so great a power as that to begin something new (Arendt, 1958: 240).

Arendt's language of "web of relations" is, I submit, her way of referring to what I called "reversibility" in the previous chapter in the following way. Like reversibility, the "web of relations" refers less to the ethical relations and more to the conditions that make ethical relations possible. That is to say, the relationship between reversibility, or the "web of relations," and forgiveness as one response to this condition, is crucial to our ability to live together in the future. This relationship can be seen when we consider how, following Desmond Tutu, forgiveness as that which unites people through practical politics emerges from the African notion of *Ubuntu*. Again, I submit that the Arendtean notion of "web of relations," and my notion of "reversibility" can be read as synonymous with *Ubuntu*. Here is how Tutu describes *Ubuntu*.

> *Ubuntu*...is difficult to render in Western languages. It speaks about the essence of being human: that my humanity is caught up in your humanity because we say a person is a person through other persons. I am a person because I belong. The same is true for

you. The solitary human being is a contradiction in terms.... No one can be fully human unless he or she relates to others in a fair, peaceful, and harmonious way. In our African understanding, we set great store by communal peace and harmony. Anything that subverts this harmony is injurious, not just to the community, but to all of us, and therefore forgiveness is an absolute necessity for continued existence (Tutu, 1998: xiii).

We can see how the Biehls witness to the interruptive power of forgiveness does so in response to the condition of reversibility. Having every right to expect reparation, they, instead, offer a new future to those who killed their daughter. In addition, they offer the families, the community, and greater South Africa the possibility of releasing itself from its past, which is to say, open it toward newness. What becomes apparent is that the web of relations, characterized in the previous chapter as reversibility, is a condition that affects Amy Biehl, her parents toward her (in that they keep her work alive), the killers and their family (a chance at newness), the community in which the Biehls and the killers and their family live (a release from this tragic event), and South Africa (a break with its criminal past). Finally, this reversibility extends to us as well, especially those of us so ingrained with retributive models of justice. Hannah Arendt saw the transformative capacity of forgiveness for politics long before recent thinkers. I mention this here because it will be important later on when I offer a response to those who are critical of the work of the TRC as abandoning Justice for Truth.

In *The Human Condition* she discusses how forgiveness is the remedy to the unpredictability of time and as such makes possible the chance to begin anew. It is in the ability to begin anew, an interruptive dimension, which best reveals the utopian character of forgiveness. In short, forgiveness undoes "the sins of the past" (Arendt, 1958: 237). This can be understood in the following manner. In many ways Arendt, foreshadowing the philosophical project of Jacques Derrida, problematizes binary oppositions inherent in the history of the Western metaphysical tradition. That is, like Derrida and others, who, in a thoroughly utopian manner undoes the sins of the past and frees the Western philosophical tradition to begin anew, Arendt captures the utopian dimension of forgiveness when she describes it as the "possible redemption from the predicament of irreversibility--of being unable to undo what one has done though one did not, and could not, have known what he was doing--is the faculty of forgiving. The remedy of unpredictability, for the chaotic certainty of the future, is contained in the faculty to make and keep promises" (Arendt, 1958: 237). As Derrida and others have shown, the Western philosophical tradition has sought to contain action and been obsessed with speaking of total presence. Philosophy as a whole, to borrow a line from John Dewey, has been preoccupied with the "quest for certainty," ahistorical universalism, complete presence, fixed order, and structures that tame the fragility of our lives, it's contingency and the abyss-like quality of human existence. Why mention this? Because traditional utopian thinking, as described in Chapter One, is a carrier of these same motivations. Thus, what is needed is to be released, as it were, from this past, which is to say, be forgiven. Without forgiveness we simply try to contain our action by rigid boundaries that, besides carrying on the sins of the past, suffocate us and render us politically and ethically impotent. The act of forgiveness illuminates, as a witness in both thought and action, a way of acting that opens us on to the world toward new possibilities. Arendt concludes:

> Without being forgiven, released from the consequences of what we have done, our capacity to act would, as it were, be confined to one single deed from which we could never recover; we would remain the victims of its consequences forever, not unlike the sorcerer's apprentice who lacked the magic formula to break the spell. Without being bound to the fulfillment of promises, we would never be able to keep our identities; *we would be condemned to wander helplessly and without direction* in the darkness of each man's lonely heart, caught in its contradictions and equivocalities... (Arendt, 1958: 237).

This Arendtian analysis prefigures those who more recently have tried to recapture the work of forgiveness in a general philosophical manner, and more specifically in terms of its importance for ethical and political life. John Caputo, in particular, can be seen within this Arendtian trajectory, on the one hand, and offering a notion of forgiveness that also resonates with that of Tutu and the TRC, on the other hand. Caputo writes:

> Forgiving keeps the web of relations loose and open-ended, making it possible for people to "change their minds" and start all over again. So if someone were to "trespass" (*harmartanein*) against you—now Arendt is commenting on an old jewgreek narrative—and then to say to you that he had a change of mind (*metanoia*), then you are to release him (*aphienai*) forgive him, forget it and release him, just the way you would want to be released if you changed your mind. Cut the cord of the past; keep no record; do not keep it in your heart (*kardia*). Cut it loose, release it. (Caputo, 1983: 111-112).

In addition, Caputo's notion of forgiveness is linked to what he calls reciprocity, but, I submit, is closer conceptually to what I call "reversibility," what Arendt calls the "web of relations," and what Tutu calls "*Ubuntu.*" According to Caputo:

> Forgiveness is the ultimate release from all economies, from every economic tie, but not into a simple exteriority from the circle. Rather, forgiving loosens the circle of credit and debt, not only from the debt that chains the other with the tie of my calculated gift, but also from the debt that makes my relation to the other one of debt. Forgiveness alone gives me responsibility without duty, duty without debt, debt without being tied up (Caputo, 1997: 227).

Even though the language is different in Caputo, his aim, along with that of Arendt and Tutu is to offer an alternative language of compassion that has tremendous ethical and political implications. More specifically, this unearthing of the potential politics of forgiveness in the work of Arendt, Caputo and the TRC is precisely that work of the utopian, in particular the importance of reversibility. In addition, what can be seen here is the way that forgiveness, as that which loosens, functions homologously to the GRACE AS GIFT metaphor in relationship the MORAL ACCOUNTING metaphor discussed in Chapter Two. The loosing in the utopian disruption that opens the potential for a new way of relating, a way that is beyond the threshold of retributive justice.

Forgiveness, in light of the above discussion, instances the element of reversibility in that, as the TRC shows, we *choose* which mode of relating we will employ in light of this condition of reversibility that is shared by victim and victimizer. In this case, we will either choose the cycle of violence that has as its central ethic retribution and revenge, or we will interrupt this cycle and choose an ethic of release, linked to the notion of forgiveness discussed above. To be sure, and realistic, in many cases what is chosen is violence because a utopian politics of forgiveness, at best, as a religious notion left for that private domain, or, at worst, not a serious category with which to structure our lived political existence characterized by violence and war. Violence is a cousin of vengeance; vengeance is the opposite of forgiveness. Forgiveness, as the TRC illustrates, provides the slack in relations that allows us to lighten up and makes possible the new possibility of existing together. Vengeance attempts containment and leads to suffocation. Forgiveness, in the way I have conceptually presented it through and engagement with Arendt and Caputo above, and the lived practices of the TRC, attempts to interrupt our standard ways of being-in-relation and offer a potentially new beginning. In this light, it is easy to see how the work of the TRC instantiates the elements of the utopian as I understand it.

Finally, the notion of forgiveness practiced by the TRC exhibits the characteristics mentioned earlier in reference to testimony. Though it makes a judgment on those ways of relating that are driven by vengeance, and is universally intended as a key for our collective living together, forgiveness perhaps most clearly parallels testimony with its emphasis on remembering. The remembering here, however, takes on a different form in that we remember the suffering perpetrated on past generations. We enter into the suffering of those who have been victims at our own hands. This kind of collective remembering recalls the struggles and triumphs of past generations, but, in order to release us to new possibilities for co-existing, it takes responsibility for calling into question those institutions and forces that seek to keep alive the instruments of affliction of past generations. By keeping alive collective memory and collective responsibility we "remember the past in order not to repeat it. We remember evil in order to build a new community with the descendants of evildoers" (Shriver, 1998: 141).[2] In this sense, we witness to forgiveness as it functions to judge the past, take account for our part in its atrocities, and keep the memory of responsibility alive for future generations. This responsible remembering, an act of a responsible witness, is described best by Tutu when he when he writes the following.:

> Forgiveness does not mean amnesia. Amnesia is a most dangerous thing, especially on a community, national, or international level. We must forgive, but almost always we should not forget that there were atrocities, because if we do, we are then likely to repeat those atrocities. Those who forgive and those who accept forgiveness must not forget in their reconciling. If we don't deal with our past adequately, it will return to haunt us. When something is unforgiven it has physical consequences for us (Tutu, 1998: xiv).

Without this kind of remembered testimony—a remembering of the struggles and responsibility—we lose the ability, as Tutu makes clear, to rid ourselves of the collective anger that will most certainly destroy us. The utopian work of forgiveness is what the TRC attempts to unearth in its political activity. In doing so, we become aware of the "*imaginaire* of rupture" as it opens to us potentially new forms of justice that are covered over in traditional forms. But it is precisely here that the utopian politics of the TRC receives its most strident criticism. The criticism, in brief, is that the utopian politics of the TRC offers an inadequate account of justice, an account that is best seen in deliberative democracy.

In what follows I take up the criticisms of two proponents of and, in turn, offer a response to their charges. My aim is two-fold. First, I want to show how the critics of the utopian politics of the TRC as I developed above are wrong in their assessment of the TRC. Second, I want to resist this criticism of the TRC because it truncates and covers the utopian potential in the work of the TRC that traditional theories, despite protests to the contrary, simply can no longer accommodate. That is to say, what the TRC offers is a possibility beyond the deadlock that is inherent in deliberative theories of justice. In the end, my goal is to keep in front of us the utopian work of the TRC, and show how its opponents miss this utopian impulse at a detriment. Before we can see this, we first must understand the project of deliberative democracy.

There is little doubt that deliberative theories of democracy dominate political thinking when it comes to living together in societies more and more characterized by the "conflict of interpretations."[3] Like many, I have become a convert to deliberative theories and embrace their possibilities to navigate such demanding pluralistic waters. But I have doubts about the capacity of deliberative theories, especially after considering more carefully an essay by two leading proponents deliberative democrats, Amy Gutmann and Dennis Thompson.

Gutmann and Thompson's essay, "The Moral Foundations of Truth Commissions," attempts to apply their version of deliberative democracy to the work of truth commissions in general and the South African Truth and Reconciliation Commission (TRC) in particular (Gutmann and Thompson, 2000).[4] After reading this article, which criticizes truth commissions as they are currently practiced and indicates how they could be corrected by deliberative theories in general and the deliberative principle of reciprocity in particular, I was concerned by how easily they could dismiss as politically legitimate a vision of society like that of the TRC simply because it did not adequately reflect an awareness with, among other things, the fundamental notion of reciprocity. With this I began thinking about what was missing in their response, and what was in the TRC that might account for this omission.

More specifically, I first want to suggest that the idea of reversibility emerges from the TRC, and more adequately reflects the lives of those involved in the TRC. Reversibility, as I argued in Chapter Four, differs from the central notion of reciprocity assumed by most if not all theories of deliberation. Second, and somewhat a result of the first, I want to maintain that the views of deliberative democracy that have reciprocity as one of their principle notions unnecessarily overemphasize the place of reciprocity ultimately at the expense of utopian movements like the TRC. Why is this notion of reciprocity so important to the deliberative democrats?

Gutmann and Thompson's insistence on reciprocity assumes, first, a strong ground of rationality, which, owing much to John Rawls, means that one's position can be presented, which is to say argued for, in a "public" (i.e., neutral) way that does not rely on particular comprehensive moral doctrines. Second, reciprocity assumes a specific logic of exchange where deliberative participants all possess the ability to rationally deliberate in proportionate ways. Finally, these two criteria work in concert to assess the moral worth of one's position, which means that reciprocal reasoning privileges the moral norm over the ethical aim where one is expected to justify their position by rational means of deliberation. Let me expand these.

There are two important points in understanding the ground of reciprocity. First, deliberative settings are governed by rational deliberation, which means "citizens and officials must justify any demands for collective action by *giving reasons* that can be accepted by those who are bound by the action" (Gutmann and Thompson, 2000: 35-36). This, in a word, is reciprocity and is "the capacity to seek fair terms of cooperation for its own sake" (Gutmann and Thompson, 1996: 52-53). As that which makes a "proportionate return for good received" reciprocity "asks citizens to try to justify their political views to one another, and to treat with respect those who make good-faith efforts to engage in this mutual enterprise even when they cannot resolve their disagreements" (Gutmann and Thompson, 2000: 36). Rational discourse, then, is synonymous with reciprocal reasoning insofar as one gives a rational account of the position in question. As they tell us, "the very activity of providing an account that other citizens can be expected to understand as reasonable (even if not right) indicates the willingness of citizens to acknowledge one another's membership in a common democratic enterprise. This is an important part of any ongoing democratic project, and therefore a step toward a democratic future in deeply divided societies" (Gutmann and Thompson, 2000: 38). As the principle that regulates rational discourse, therefore, reciprocity is claimed to shape public interaction, influence the understanding of liberty and opportunity offered and, most importantly express a sense of mutuality that guides proceedings that allows for a wide range of reasonable disagreement. If, in the end, one's argument or principle(s) cannot be mutually "accessible" to fellow citizens, then one fails at reciprocal reasoning, which is a failure to justify one's position. Thus, Gutmann and Thompson conclude, "Any claim fails to respect reciprocity if it imposes a requirement on other citizens to adopt one's sectarian way of life as a condition for gaining access to the moral understanding that is essential to judging the validity of one's moral claims" (Gutmann and Thompson, 1996: 57). It is no surprise, seen in this light, that reciprocity operates on a particular logic.

The logic of reciprocity is revealed clearly when Gutmann and Thompson tell us explicitly that reciprocity makes "proportionate return for the good received" (2000: 36). Linked to one's ability to make rationally accessible the position in question, the assumption here is that each individual has similar capacities to generate rational arguments that present their positions to other deliberative participants who themselves share the similar capacities and who, presumably, can recognize the validity of arguments and counter arguments even though they may disagree and reject with them. The logic of reciprocity, as this discussion reveals, is one of exchange. To be sure, Gutmann and Thompson do not mean to suggest that everyone will agree only that good deliberative citizens will be able to present the *substance* of their positions (contra Habermas on their understanding) in mutually accessible ways to other rational participants who possess a similar capacity. Together the ground of rationality and the logic of reciprocal exchange provide the framework whereby we are able to justify the moral worth of our position. That is to say, proceeding along the lines of reciprocity enables one to ask whether or not a particular position is morally *justified*. Thus, reciprocity guarantees that moral justification will be preferred. Here is what I mean by this.

The fundamental moral requirement of reciprocity is three-fold and must be met if a position is to be considered as a legitimate part of the political agenda of society. First, the position must be moral in principle, which means it should "explicitly appeal to rights or goods that are moral and therefore are comparable to the justice that is being sacrificed" (Gutmann and Thompson, 2000: 23). This challenge calls on those who defend the aims and activities of a particular movement or position to distinguish it as morally justified from a purely prudential or self- or group- interested one. Second, it must be moral in perspective, which is to say otherwise that it will offer reasons that are as far as possible broadly accessible and therefore inclusive of as many people as possible who seek moral terms of social cooperation. Finally, if a position is to be morally justified it will be moral in practice, which means that the position will practice "what it preaches about the democratic society it is trying to help create" (Gutmann and Thompson, 2000: 37). And what happens if a position omits reciprocal reasoning? Does this mean that one's position is *a priori* morally unjustified if it does not contain the three moral criteria? Here we have to venture an interpretation of Gutmann and Thompson.

On the one hand, if reciprocal reasoning is omitted either explicitly or implicitly, then the position offered is at best incomplete. On the other hand, if reciprocity is unaccounted for in the specific ways mentioned by Gutmann and Thompson, especially the three-fold criteria of meeting the moral requirement, and the position in question is demanded to be adopted by it proponents, then what results is a position that "imposes a requirement on other citizens" that cannot be rationally accepted by other rational agents and this makes the position tyrannical. Here is where their reading of the TRC is especially troubling. Before I suggest more clearly what is troubling about this proposal, let us first consider what Gutmann and Thompson have to say about the relationship between deliberative democracy and truth commissions in general.

It is no surprise that Gutmann and Thompson believe deliberative democracy best addresses the place of truth commissions in general and the TRC in particular in democracies. They write:

> In justifying truth commissions in a democratic context, we rely on a deliberative democracy. Deliberative democracy offers the most perspective by which to judge the work of truth commissions that engage in public deliberations because, more than other conceptions of democracy, it defends a deliberative politics that is explicitly designed to deal with ongoing moral controversy. At the core of deliberative democracy is the idea that citizens and officials must justify any demands for collective action by giving reasons that can be accepted by those who are bound by the action ...The fundamental value underlying this conception is reciprocity, which asks citizens to try to justify their political views to one another, and to treat with respect those who make good-faith efforts to engage in this mutual enterprise even when they cannot resolve their disagreements (Gutmann and Thompson, 2000: 35).

This means, then, that the moral burden of the TRC is to give a rational account as to why for Gutmann and Thompson, it sacrifices the pursuit of justice as usually understood and favors the promotion of other social purposes, such as historical truth and social reconciliation. Accordingly, if justice is sacrificed on their reading so is reciprocity because reciprocity and justice are integrally related and the omission of one means the sacrifice of the other. If we remember that reciprocity expresses both a rationally acceptable and subsequent morally justified position that, while not necessarily being adopted by other, could be accepted rationally, then failure to appropriately practice reciprocity means, I suggest, that the position in question when persisted on is morally unjustified. Put bluntly, if the TRC is to be a legitimate option in a democratic society structured by deliberation, then the TRC must model reciprocity. In addition, if it is to be morally justified then it must meet all three of the moral criteria mentioned above. Failure to do so, coupled with the insistence on one's commitment to a position that meets at best only some of the criteria has to mean that the position in question is morally unjustified because only reciprocity as understood by deliberative democrats like Gutmann and Thompson satisfactorily meets the moral burden of justifying truth commissions. For the TRC to be a legitimate option in democratic politics it must provide a rational account acceptable to all people though the proposal may certainly be rejected. If it meets this burden, which is practicing reciprocity, then the vision of the TRC is morally justified. What then are we to make of the TRC as it was practiced?

One way of reading Gutmann and Thompson here is to see them saying that the TRC is incomplete because it relies too heavily on comprehensive commitments such as forgiveness that consequently delegitimize it for a deliberative democratic politics. What happens, however, when proponents of the TRC insist that "without forgiveness there is no future" where the implication is that South Africa cannot deal with its past via "usually understood" views of justice, like those assumed by Gutmann and Thompson (and most deliberative theorists)? What happens when, in the words of one prominent South African political theorist, there is a conscious decision to make it clear that truth commissions like the one in South Africa "differ from tribunals in giving priority to hearings in which the victims can tell their own stories, rather than seeking the prosecution and punishment of perpetrators. This implies a choice for "truth" (of victims) over (retributive) justice" (Du Toit, 2000: 127). Here is where the predicament emerges for me.

A strict reading of Gutmann and Thompson's view of reciprocity creates a dilemma for us. To their credit, they acknowledge first that truth commissions in general and the TRC in particular exhibit some of the moral requirements of reciprocity, but as currently understood do not fully embody reciprocal reasoning. Second, as I say above, they acknowledge that such movements could, in theory, adopt reciprocal reasoning, which would move them beyond the limits of comprehensive moral frameworks and thus position them as legitimate options in a democratic society. Remember, however, if the TRC is to make such a move then it would have to embody reciprocity in a way that Gutmann and Thompson demand otherwise the TRC only partially exercises reciprocity. While I want to give Gutmann and Thompson proper credit here, their gestures, I suggest, are finally misleading. Let us ask whether or not in light of the view of reciprocity offered, especially its attending emphasis on meeting the three-fold moral requirement that justifies a position as politically legitimate in a democratic society, the TRC with its insistence on forgiveness and reconciliation is in the end morally unjustified? Commitment to anything else like forgiveness and reconciliation at best only partially fulfills the requirements of reciprocity and further insistence on comprehensive positions ultimately deems the TRC morally unjustified and inappropriate as a political option in a democratic society tied to deliberative theories of reciprocal reasoning. What, then, are we to do?

One response is that Gutmann and Thompson are correct and *only* reciprocity as the mode by which we make rationally accessible our own positions can do this work of legitimacy, and the TRC, like other positions based on comprehensive frameworks, is illegitimate insofar as it does not adopt fully the dimensions of reciprocity. Another response is to see the emphasis on reciprocity as an overemphasis that hides a more fundamental notion that not only challenges the way reciprocity overreaches, but also a more fundamental notion makes reciprocal reasoning possible. I want to take this latter position and claim that reversibility is such a concept.

To help us raise the possibility of reversibility, I want to ask the following questions. First, is reciprocity the only way to understand what it means to "give an account" of one's position? To take the example of the TRC, what happens to the victims (as well as victimizers) of Apartheid who cannot give the kinds of reason that a notion like reciprocity requires? Do they have no place in the discourse concerning justice relative to fashioning a future beyond atrocious frameworks like Apartheid? More pointedly, can those who themselves have died for the vision of the TRC be taken seriously with regards to questions of justice if they literally can no longer offer reasons? (I will return to this below).

To argue for the notion of reversibility as being the best way to understand the work of the TRC, I want to utilize a specific instance relative to the TRC that demonstrates something other to reciprocity. Under the sign of reversibility I want to present an understanding of how victims and victimizers, self and other, coexist symbiotically and what is demanded is not a morally justified principle that works to procure rational agreement between us (though this would not be precluded), but a demand to the response *before* reciprocity is chosen that makes moral reasoning possible. In addition, I want to suggest that reversibility best captures what happens *after* the moral principle of reciprocity fails us.

This is similar to the point I made in relationship to Cornel West that "we are not connected in ways that we would like to be but also, in a more profound sense, ...this failure to connect binds us even more tightly together" and that either "we learn a new language of empathy and compassion, or the fire this time will consume us all" (West, 1994: 8; 13). To augment this, let me borrow and extend an idea from Stanley Cavell, who says that we are both separated and together— *for no reason* (see Cavell, 1979). The concept that best represents these ideas is reversibility.

Recall also that in Chapter Four I argued that reversibility is the condition of both being-together and remaining apart that signifies not only the fundamental ways that humans are intertwined together, but also equally the distance that exists between them. As such reversibility illuminates for us the importance of a response before moral norms, but equally the ways in which our responses take on the form of violence. To develop this in conjunction with the work of the TRC I want to follow the line of thinking I did with reciprocity. Accordingly, let us begin with the ground and logic of reversibility.

As a condition for both the possibility of reciprocity and equally the condition for violence, reversibility is, first, *phenomenologically grounded* in the lived experiences of humans, especially those experiences that mark their lives in fundamental ways. As such, reversibility de-emphasizes, we might say, the need for a strong view of rationality and emphasizes more the concrete lived experiences of those thrown into and affected by situations. To claim that reversibility has a phenomenological rather than epistemic ground is to suggest, second, that there is a fundamental intertwinement between my lived experience and the experience of others in an intertwinement that opens the possibility for response that comes prior to moral norms and exceeds them when they fail. As I said above, that reversibility resonates with *Ubuntu*. As that which illuminates this primordial condition, reversibility makes both responses possible and a moral response like reciprocity already assumes reversibility. It is here, in particular, that we begin to see more clearly how reversibility signifies the *before* that makes something like reciprocity possible and the *after* that emerges in the failure of moral principles like reciprocity. So let me begin with the before.

Reversibility is the condition of being-together and remaining apart that signifies to us this fundamental intertwinement to which our decisions (reciprocity or otherwise) respond. When I say we are in a stance of reversibility, I mean simply that our futures and in some real sense our pasts are linked though we may never come into literal contact. While this may be a trivial notion, it is a condition that is often forgotten and returns only when something tragic occurs. One need only to think of how a tragedy like September 11 reveals the way we are in a reversible stance with those who, in this case, sought to destroy us. Our futures, like our pasts to some degree, are forever linked and reciprocity as a way of opening the channels of closed dialogue is only one potential made possible by the awareness that our lives in America are forever intertwined with those in the Middle East. This is not to say we have never known this but that the events of September 11 reveal to us something we have forgotten, namely, that we are, in the words of Cornel West, "not connected in ways that we would like to be but also, in a more profound sense...this failure to connect binds us even more tightly together." In addition, these events reveal to us how the condition of reversibility still demands to be recognized long after the concept of reciprocity fails to do what its proponents would like, namely, procure *rational* agreement so that such events like September 11 might be avoided. This, again, is not to diminish the place of reciprocity in deliberation but rather to point out that it, like other moral criteria, fails us and that we find ourselves intertwined nevertheless with those who, in this case, reject the moral criterion of reciprocity. And, following Cavell once more, we find ourselves *after the failure of* these criteria intertwined with others *for no reason*.

It is in this light that I want to say with great trepidation that reversibility strikes me as more "value-free," than reciprocity insofar as reversibility is neither inherently good nor bad, but rather the condition for both. We would say, for example, that our response to the condition of reversibility is good if we reciprocate and do not kill each other. We would say that our response is bad if, after we became aware of this condition that we decide the other with whom we are intertwined is unworthy of reciprocation and therefore seek to exclude or even kill them. Put differently, reversibility as the before is the acknowledgement that you and I are intertwined and that you are either worthy of reciprocation or worthy of killing. Reciprocity occurs as only one particular response to this before that opens the possibility of multiple responses. Now let me address the after, which I find more pertinent to Gutmann and Thompson.

What are we to do when reciprocity in particular fails us (as Gutmann and Thompson themselves acknowledge)? One response is to deem such participants morally unjustified because they lack reciprocity. And, we should add, that one is justified in excluding such positions from political discourse, because political legitimacy is tied directly to one's ability to exhibit reciprocal reasoning. While this may work in many cases, and I have my doubts, the need to have *ethical relations* with those who, let's assume, do not have a morally justified position still exists. That is to say, long after reciprocity fails us we are still faced with the need to respond to those who, to be honest, could not care less about reciprocity. Adopting a notion of reversibility, I suggest, better helps us to understand this situation though it in no way suggests any more agreement than reciprocity does. My point here is that reversibility helps us to see that you can have the best kinds of procedures—substantive or otherwise—that function to justify at least whether or not one is at least a reasonable participant. If, however, such procedures fail, and they do, we are still left with a decision to respond to the condition that we are both separate and together—for no reason. Here I will say is where we begin to see how reversibility privileges an ethical relation over the moral norm of reciprocity and also reveals a different logic.

Instead of the logic of exchange, which in reciprocal reason is discussed in terms of proportionality, reversibility, along the lines of the TRC's insistence on forgiveness, assumes the importance of giving. It is worth noting here that the argument in Chapter Two where I showed the interruptive potential of GRACE AS GIFT to the MORAL ACCOUNTING metaphor is applicable as well. My aim here, however, is to situate this assumption of giving relative to Gutmann and Thompson. Recall for them that reciprocity as a dimension of justice makes "a proportionate return for the good received," which is to say that the logic of reciprocity depends on the notion of exchange. And to give an account of oneself is to do so along these proportionate lines reflected in one's ability to present their position in mutually accessible ways. Reversibility, however, affords us an alternative understanding of what it means to "give an account of."

First, instead of giving an account that moves from premises to conclusions and ones that appeal solely to the best empirical research, reversibility allows for the other ways we use to open our positions. To give an account under the sign of reversibility is, as the Biehls attest, to witness to one's experience with the goal of making available one's position beyond the confines of rational argumentation. To be sure, this does not mean we reject rational argument, only that often more is needed to give an account of one's lived experience.

Second, and related, reversibility as giving of one's testimony is especially important for understanding how those who may not be able to reciprocate or cannot do so are still able to give an account of their position, where giving an account as witnessing opens the door to new ways of responding to the condition that binds and separates us. This point is made poignantly in the work of the TRC. To emphasize, many people simply cannot engage in the kind of reciprocal reasoning where they give back what is proportionate. Yet these people do present a position that, while not meeting the strict definition of reciprocity, nevertheless provides us with a view that instead of sacrificing justice for truth, as is the criticism of Gutmann and Thompson, opens to us a new paradigm of justice itself. The entire story of Amy Biehl and all that emerged around her death is precisely about the work that takes place in the face of a deadlock that has emerged because of our adherence to a way of thinking that no longer functions for us the way it once might have.

Amy Biehl was literally unable to give an account of herself and engage in reciprocal reasoning. Yet, she gave an account of herself in a way that not only transformed the situation in which she lived and died, but radically altered the lives of her parents. We could say that Amy's parent's actions did not so much as argue for the position their daughter professed, but rather testified both to the work of their daughter and by extension to the transformative power of the TRC. The Biehls continued Amy's work in South Africa so that the work of healing and reconciliation, the work of justice, can continue, albeit beyond the paradigm of reciprocity as envisioned by Gutmann and Thompson. I am suggesting, in the end, that this story cannot be adequately understood under the sign of reciprocity as Gutmann and Thompson argue for it, but rather illustrates the ways in which reciprocity as a moral principle fails us and calls for ethical relations after this failure. This story, further illustrates the notion of reversibility that makes reciprocity possible and illustrates again how the condition of reversibility emerges after reciprocity fails us, carrying with it the utopian potential hidden by reciprocity. What is privileged is a call to ethical relations beyond the demand for moral justification. This is not to say that by privileging the call to ethical relations that we dispense with moral justification inherent in the notion of reciprocity. Instead, it is simply to demonstrate how, on the one hand, reciprocity and the logic entailed by it can and often does become an overemphasized notion at the expense of the lived bodily experience of those demanded to reciprocate. On the other hand, the privileging of the ethical relations that emerge from a logic of reversibility, rooted in the phenomenological dimensions of existence—and here the language of privilege is admittedly problematic—is to call for more consideration of that which makes reciprocity possible and that notion which exists after reciprocity. It is to account for reversibility. Taking reversibility seriously as a phenomenological ground that operates on a different logic of giving an account of oneself can ultimately enrich our understanding of deliberation, which as it stands can no longer deliver on its promises.

In this chapter, I have tried to indicate how the TRC exemplifies the elements of the utopian that I have been developing throughout. With its insistence on forgiveness, the TRC offers a way of being together that interrupts our most cherished understanding of justice based on a deliberative framework. The emphasis here should be placed on the interruption because, as I argued in Chapter Two with regards to grace, the interruption occurs *within* a framework and emerges in a dialectical relation with that it seeks to interrupt. This is exactly what went on with the TRC and the Biehls who embraced this work. This is not to say that either the TRC or I am suggesting we throw deliberative democracy out the window. It is, instead, to say that a utopian politics of disruption like that of the TRC (and other examples I have mentioned) is a reminder of how our positions, policies, understandings and so forth have the potential, in the name of liberation, to suffocate the emancipatory spirit. This inability to allow for the utopian, as I have argued above, is what occurs when deliberative democrats dismiss the universal liberatory spirit alive in the work of the TRC and its utopian politics. What I have suggested is that discerning the utopian might be less about the vision toward which we are moving, or the process that gets us there, and more about the way the utopian as a work of imaginative interruption calls us to engage the world once again in the name of universal emancipation. This kind of work is more relevant than ever and is, truly, a moral imperative.

Notes

Notes to chapter one

1. Though I will utilize the phenomenology of Merleau-Ponty, one can easily detect a Heideggerian connection with the idea of retrieval. I am thinking especially of the following passage from *An Introduction to Metaphysics* where, in speaking of retrieval (*Wiederholung*), Heidegger writes that retrieval is a drawing out of new possibilities from old origins and that something retrieved "can be preserved only by re-trieving it its originality more originally." Thus, he concludes, retrieval "as we understand it is anything but a better way of continuing the past by the methods of the past." See Heidegger (1959: 39; 191).

2. I have not been able to locate sustained arguments against utopian thinking by feminist theorists. At best what emerges is a traditional understanding of utopian thought, and a good example of the tacit critique mentioned earlier, as that which captures all utopian thinking. This traditional understanding can be found in almost all references to utopian thought, for example, as when Iris Young (1990a: 103), in writing about the impossibility of adopting a point of view dislocated from context, says "such a notion of moral reason in philosophy is *utopian*," which I believe assumes an homogeneous understanding of utopian thinking. I say assume here because there is no further attempt by Young (or others for that matter) to acknowledge another history, as it were, of utopian thought.

Though I mention Benhabib and Moi, who represent the philosophical traditions of critical theory and poststructuralism respectively, Drucilla Cornell has for some time now been a lone voice in the postmodern desert crying out for the necessity of the utopian mentality. This theme, though not thoroughly developed, receives mention in virtually all of her work. See especially (Cornell, 1991 and 1992) where she continues to press this theme when she writes that the "politics of utopian possibility," understood as the "not-yet" is that mode of thought and action that "keeps open the 'beyond' of currently unimaginable transformative possibilities" (1992: 182, *passim*).

3. I borrow this heuristic from the work of Ruth Levitas (1990).

4. This idea is expressed in virtually all extended discussions of utopian thought. For two good accounts that give detail to this notion see Kumar (1991), and the classic Manuel and Manuel, (1979).

Notes to chapter two

1. I am indebted to Slavoj Žižek for helping me think about this point. See Žižek (2008).

2. Though I came to this idea of the utopian as an advent on my own I have had the fortune of finding a similar position in William Desmond whose work has deepened my own understanding of this matter. I am particularly indebted to the way he writes of the advent with regards to metaphysical thinking. In the discussion what follows, therefore, I employ Desmond (1995) at key points.

3. Jacques Derrida and John Caputo have influenced my thinking about the utopian as impossible.

4. Again, I wish to acknowledge the work of William Desmond (1995), whose insights regarding Plato have helped shaped this discussion here, especially with regards to understanding what I here call the double meaning of the utopian.

5. The following account for the MORAL ACCOUNTING metaphor is adapted from Mark Johnson (1993: 45).

6. Let me make something clear. The use of "law" here is not meant to put forth a theological claim opposing Jesus to the Torah. Rather, my point is to suggest, via a reference to linguistic evidence as understood from the methodological commitments of cognitive linguistics that this idea of "law," and the adherence to or breaking of it, is a way of conceptualizing receiving a gift we deserve. On the one hand, if we "break the law," God's or human's, then "we get what we *deserve.*" It is a form of retributive justice at work. If, on the other hand, we break the law and get grace, that is, get something we do not deserve, then a virtual frenzy ensues. One need only witness the many death row inmates in the United States who get commuted sentences, for example, to the great protest of many. Why such protest? These criminals, so the argument goes, are not "paying the price" for their actions, which is to say, they are not getting what they deserve, or retribution is being surpassed for a form of response that, understood relative to a retributive model, seems ludicrous.

Notes to chapter three

1. Robert Bernasconi (2000) presents a compelling account of how the future of Continental philosophy might or should be tied to the movement of phenomenology.

2. Let me note here that Critchley's claim about Continental philosophy

and the utopian is not simply an idiosyncratic reading of this tradition. There is more evidence from Continental philosophers in general and phenomenologists in particular that support Critchley's claim and my overall argument. First, Paul Ricoeur's work (1986) on the utopian is a model not the least of which is his own orientation as a phenomenologist. With this said, I would still maintain that ultimately his work focuses on thinkers aligned more with critical theory than phenomenology (e.g., Marx and Habermas). Second and perhaps more indirectly, I would again mention the exemplary work of Robert Bernasconi who reveals what could be considered to be a utopian dimension to phenomenology when he writes, "The phenomenological movement can itself be understood as a tradition that opens the future and does not merely open onto the future. Phenomenology has from the outset been experienced as a breath of fresh air" (Bernasconi, 2000: 3). Both Ricoeur and Bernasconi echo Critchley's claim and offer further evidence why Critchley's statement is in the end worth further consideration.

3. This aversion to the utopian cuts across philosophical orientations. While my interest in this chapter is with the Continental tradition, the same need to distance oneself from the utopian occurs as often in Anglo-American philosophy. Here is just one instance. Thomas Hill, Jr., whose work on Kant's ethics is exceptional, cautions us against reading Kant's kingdom of ends formula of the categorical imperative as utopian. I am not concerned with his interpretation of Kant. Instead, I am more interested in the way that the utopian is characterized. He begins by telling us that the "kingdom of ends principle, unless qualified, is in danger, of encouraging *utopian* thinking" (emphasis in original). What, then, does this mean? He continues: "That is, unless we are wary, it may lead us to draw unreasonable inferences about how we should act in our very *imperfect* world from our thought experiments about ideal agents in a *more perfect world* (Hill, Jr. 2000: 53. Emphasis added). Very little is said about the utopian, but what I say of Derrida and Irigaray applies as well to Hill, namely, that what is said clearly betrays an understanding, or better an assumption, that the utopian is opposed to our situations and as such must be avoided. It is a view that is pervasive throughout philosophy and why such an understanding can accurately be defined as conventional.

4. I have in mind here two claims made by Gary Madison in his book *The Hermeneutics of Postmodernity: Figures and Themes* (Madison, 1988). First, that at the end of his life Merleau-Ponty "absolutely did not subscribe to utopianism and abandoned whatever belief he might have had in the possibility of some kind of definitive resolution of the differences

and conflicts that separate people, and this, of course, is why he clearly took his distance from Marxism." (72). Second, Merleau-Ponty's turn away from utopian thinking is a turn toward the reaffirmation of history. Thus, according to Madison, this amounts to a "rejection of the utopian belief in some kind of trans- or metahistorical salvation, the desire, the avowed, or unavowed, on the part of much of postmodernity for a saving god, for the overcoming of all alienation." (73). Even though Madison, in my estimation, is one of the more astute Merleau-Ponty interpreters, his point regarding utopian thinking as it stands in relation to Merleau-Ponty is wrongheaded because it presumes all utopian thinking is the same, i.e., of the conventional sort.

5. I am indebted to the work of others in developing some of my thinking in this regard. In particular, I have benefited from the work of Lorraine Code (1991), Mark Johnson, (1989); and Michael Polanyi, (1962).

6. See Emmanuel Levinas (1981). The principal way it is used in contemporary discourse is to begin with a theory about ethical life (such as deontology, utilitarianism, etc), get this theory clearly delineated (for instance, what is proper consent, responsibility, etc), and then apply this line of thinking to a variety of issues (such as war). This latter move, in effect, is what in most contemporary versions makes applied ethics politics and constitutes the prevailing contemporary understanding of practical philosophy.

7. I borrow this term from Jacques Derrida and John Caputo.

8. See especially the Introduction to *Phenomenology of Perception*. All other references to this text will be noted by "PhP" followed by the page number. For a helpful commentary on this paradox of transcendence and immanence as Merleau-Ponty's response engages Sartre, see Dillon (1988), especially chapter 2.

9. This understanding of transcendence influences Merleau-Ponty's view of history as well. In the passage following this phrase he writes the following.

> Furthermore, no philosophy of history has ever carried all the substance of the present over into the future or *destroyed* the self to make room for the other person. Such a neurotic attitude toward the future would be exactly non-philosophy, the deliberate refusal to know what one believes in. No philosophy has ever consisted in choosing between transcendences—for example between that of God and that of a human future. They have all been concerned with mediating them . . . and with

elucidating that stance enveloping movement [my emphasis] which makes the choice of means already a choice of ends and the self become world cultural history (Ibid).

See also (1969b) for more on his view of history.
10. The term "epidermalizing" is borrowed from Thomas Slaughter's "Epidermalizing the World: A Basic Mode of Being Black," in Harris, (1984). I owe the discovery of this term to Iris Young, whose work has influenced my argument on this point.

Notes to chapter four

1. The passage in reference is section forty of Kant's *Critique of Judgment* (Kant, 1987: 160) where he says: "[Let us compare with the *sensus communis*] the common human understanding, even though the latter is not being included here as a part of the critique of taste. The following maxims may serve to elucidate its principles: (1) to think for oneself; (2) to think from the standpoint of everyone else; and (3) to think always consistently.
It should be noted that my intent here is not to argue either for this reading of Kant or assess Arendt's interpretation. Rather, I am concerned only with showing Arendt's interest in this concept of enlarged thought and how it has resurfaced in recent political exchanges.
2. See also Bernstein's helpful chapter "Judging—The Actor and the Spectator," in (Bernstein, 1986).
3. Arendt as both influence and dialogue partner is present in Benhabib's early work (1986), given its fullest consideration in (1992), and is still an interest, albeit of less focus, (1996). In her most recent work (2008), the notion of reversibility is not explicitly taken up as it is in earlier works, but the notion hovers in this work, if only in a presupposed manner, with her discussion of hospitality and international or global citizenship.
4. The ideal of "overlapping consensus" is pursued throughout Rawls's writings. See especially (1993).
5. In his early work, *Theory of Justice,* Rawls (1974) is a good example. He seeks to modify this position in *Political Liberalism*, however. The best example is Bruce Ackerman who proposes what "conversational restraint," which he describes in the following way.

When you and I learn that we disagree about one another dimension of the moral truth, we should not search for some common value that will trump this disagreement; nor should we try to translate our moral disagreement into some putatively neutral framework; nor should we seek to transcend our disagreement by talking about how some hypothetical creature would resolve it. *We should simply say nothing at all about this disagreement* and try to solve our problem by invoking premises that we do agree upon. In restraining ourselves in this way, we need not lose the chance to talk to one another about our deepest, moral disagreements in countless other, more private, contexts. Having constrained the conversation in this way, we may instead use dialogue for pragmatically productive purposes: to identify normative premises all political participants find reasonable (or, at least, not unreasonable) (Ackerman, 1989: 16-17), as quoted in Benhabib, (1992, 96-97).

6. Young's fuller account of asymmetrical reciprocity can be found in her article "Asymmetrical Reciprocity: On Moral Respect, Wonder, and Enlarged Thought," (Young, 1997b).
7. Hereafter VI.
8. Hereafter, PP.
9. I have not mentioned the specific connection with Merleau-Ponty's discussion of "chiasm." Since the discussion of the relationship between chiasm and reversibility would be altogether different, I have chosen not to pursue it here.
10. Further references to Reagon will be noted parenthetically. I am indebted to Romand Coles for bringing to my attention the work of Bernice Reagon. See Coles, (1997).

Notes to chapter five

1. This is a term of Michael Polanyi (see, for example 1962). I came to Polanyi through the work of Jerry Gill (see 1981 and 2000).
2. I should add that even though the language of "new universalism" is used here, it is not entirely accurate. The history of Western philosophy possesses varied thinkers whose work both directly and indirectly reflects a different, more participatory or situated view of universalism. A "new universalism" is as old as philosophy itself. For example, Heraclitus' work could be considered the foundations for such a view, whereas Hegel, Merleau-Ponty and John Dewey (1988) all provide rich understandings of universalism that are anything but traditional. The reader who is interested

in pursuing this line of argument should consult the following. I would say that this feminist account of universalism adds the insistence that the particularity of the experience of women in the South Caucus is the key to understanding where the universal impetus lies. Anyone familiar with Hegel knows this is a point made throughout *The Phenomenology of Spirit*.

3. A classic example of this would be Jean-Jacques Rousseau, *The Social Contract*.

4. See Kierkegaard (1983).

5. I am indebted to Williams, though I am not interested in the multi-layered argument of his position (as remarkable as it is). Instead, I am interested in the way a witness who is *responsible* practices sincerity and accuracy in the basic way that Williams suggests. For a Williams full proposal see (Williams, 2002).

Notes to chapter six

1. All references that follow are to this interview.

2. Shriver (1998 and 1996) has helped me to think about the connections of forgiveness to the dimensions of judgment and universal intent.

3. This is Paul Ricoeur's phrase.

4. Gutmann and Thompson delineate more extensively the notion of reciprocity in the book that precedes this essay. See Gutmann and Thompson (1996). I will focus on the essay and, where appropriate draw on the book.

Bibliography

Ackerman, Bruce. 1989. "Why Dialogue?" *Journal of Philosophy*. 86 (January): 1-33.

Arendt, Hannah. 1982. *Lectures on Kant's Political Philosophy*. Chicago: University of Chicago Press.

———. 1963. *Eichmann in Jerusalem: A Report on the Banality of Evil*. New York: Penguin Press.

———. 1961. *Between Past and Future*. New York: Penguin Press.

———. 1958. *The Human Condition*. Chicago: University of Chicago Press.

Badiou, Alain. 2008. *Saint Paul: The Foundation of Universalism*. Translated by Ray Brassier. Palo Alto: Stanford University Press.

Benhabib, Seyla. 2008. *Another Cosmopolitanism*. Oxford and New York: Oxford University Press.

———. 1996a. *The Reluctant Modernism of Hannah Arendt*. Thousand Oaks, California: Sage Publication.

———. 1996b. "Toward a Deliberative Model of Democratic Legitimacy." In *Democracy and Difference: Contesting the Boundaries of the Political*. Ed. Seyla Benhabib. Princeton, NJ: Princeton University Press.

———. 1994. "In Defense of Universalism---Yet Again! A Response to Critics of Situating the Self." *New German Critique*. 62 (Spring-Summer): 15-30.

———. 1992. *Situating the Self*. New York: Routledge.

———. 1986. *Critique, Norm, and Utopia*. New York: Columbia University Press.

Bernasconi, Robert. 2000. "Almost Always More Than Philosophy Proper." *Research in Phenomenology*. 30, No. 1: 1-11

Bernstein, Richard J. 1986. *Philosophical Profiles*. Philadelphia: University of Pennsylvania Press.

———. 1983. *Beyond Objectivism and Relativism*. Philadelphia: University of Pennsylvania Press.

Biehl, John and Mary. 1999. *60 Minutes*, interviewed by Ed Bradley (January 16).

Bonhoeffer, Ditrich. 1961. *The Cost of Discipleship*. New York: Harper & Row.

Boff, Leonardo. 1979. *Liberating Grace*. New York: Orbis Press.

Caputo, John. 1997. *The Prayers and Tears of Jacques Derrida: Religion Without Religion*. Bloomington and Indianapolis: Indiana University Press.

———. 1983. *Against Ethics: Contribution to a Poetics of Obligation with Constant Reference to Deconstruction*. Bloomington and Indianapolis: Indiana University Press.

Cavell, Stanley. 1979. *The Claim of Reason: Wittgenstein, Skepticism, Morality, and Tragedy*. Oxford and New York: Oxford University Press.

Code, Lorraine. 1991. *What Can She Know?: Feminist Theory and the Construction of Knowledge*. Ithaca: Cornell University Press.

Colapietro, Vincent. 1998. "Entangling Alliances and Critical Traditions: Reclaiming the Possibilities of Critique." *The Journal of Speculative Philosophy*. 12, No. 2: 1-23.

Coles, Romand. 1997. *Rethinking Generosity: Critical Theory and the Politics of Caritas*. Ithaca: Cornell University Press.

Collins, Patricia Hill. 1990. *Black Feminist Thought: Knowledge, Consciousness and the Politics of Empowerment*. London: HarperCollins.

Cornell, Drucilla. 1998. *At the Heart of Freedom: Feminism, Sex, & Equality*. New Jersey: Princeton University Press.

———. 1992. *The Philosophy of the Limit*. New York: Routledge.

———. 1991. *Beyond Accommodation: Ethical Feminism, Deconstruction, and the Law*. New York: Routledge Press

Critchley, Simon. 2007. *Infinitely Demanding: Ethics of Commitment, Politics of Resistance*. New York: Verso Press.

———. 1998a. *"What is Continental Philosophy?" A Companion to Continental Philosophy*. Edited by S. Critchley and W. Schroeder. Oxford and New York: Blackwell Publishers.

––––––. 1998b. *On Derrida's Specters of Marx*. Philosophy and Social Criticism 21 (3).

D'Souza, Corinne Kumar. 1992. "The South Wind." *Terra Femina*, Brazil. Edited by Rosiska Darcy de Oliviera and Thais Corral. Institute of Cultural Action.

Dahrendorf, Ralf. 1990. *Reflections on the Revolution in Europe*. New York: Random House.

Derrida, Jacques. 200. *Negotiations: Interventions and Interviews, 1971-2001*. Palo Alto: Stanford University Press.

––––––. 1995. *On the Name*. Edited by Thomas Dutoit. Palo Alto: Stanford University Press.

––––––. 1994. *The Specters of Marx: The State of the Debt, the Work of Mourning, and the New International*. Translated by Peggy Kamuf. New York: Routledge Press.

Desmond, William. 1995. *Being and the Between*. Albany: State University of New York Press.

Dewey, John. 1988. *The Quest for Certainty: The Later Works, 1925-1953*. Edited by Jo Ann Boydston. Carbondale: Southern Illinois University Press.

Dillon, M.C. 1988. *Merleau-Ponty's Ontology*. Bloomington and Indianapolis: Indiana University Press.

Donskis, Leonidis. 1996. "The End of Utopia?" *Soundings: An Interdisciplinary Journal*. 79, No. 1-2 (Spring/Summer): 110-135.

Du Toit, André. 2000. "The Moral Foundations of the South African TRC: Truth as Acknowledgment and Justice as Recognition." In *Truth v. Justice*. Edited by Robert Rotberg and Dennis Thompson. New Jersey: Princeton University Press.

Frye, Northrop. 1966. "Varieties of Literary Utopias." In *Utopias and Utopian Thought*. Edited by Frank Manuel and Fritzie Manuel. Boston: Houghton-Mifflin.

Gibbs, Raymond. 1994. *The Poetics of Mind: Figurative Thought, Language, and Understanding*. Cambridge: Cambridge University Press.

Gill, Jerry H. 2000. *The Tacit Mode: Michael Polanyi's Postmodern Philosophy*. New York: State University of New York Press.

―――. 1991. *Merleau-Ponty and Metaphor*. Atlantic Highlands: Humanities Press.

―――. 1981. *On Knowing God*. Louisville: Westminster Press.

Goodwin, Barbara. 1991. "Utopianism." *The Blackwell Encyclopedia of Political Thought*. Edited by David Miller. Oxford: Basil Blackwell.

―――. 1978. *Social Science and Utopia: Nineteenth Century Models of Social Harmony*. Brighton: Harvester Press.

Guignon, Charles and Derk Pereboom. 2001. *Existentialism: Basic Writings*. Indianapolis: Hackett Publishing.

Gutmann, Amy and Dennis Thompson. 2000. "The Moral Foundation of Truth Commissions." In *Truth v. Justice*. Edited by Robert Rotberg and Dennis Thompson. New Jersey: Princeton University Press.

―――. 1996. *Democracy and Disagreement*. Cambridge, MA: Harvard University Press.

Habel, Norman. 1992. "In Defense of God the Sage." In *The Voice from the Whirlwind: Interpreting the Book of Job*. Edited by L.G. Perdue & W.C. Gilpin. Nashville: Abingdon Press.

Harris, Leonard. Editor. 1984. *Philosophy Born of Struggle*. Dubuque: Hunt Press.

Heidegger, Martin. 1959. *An Introduction to Metaphysics*. Translated by Ralph Manheim. New Haven: Yale University Press.

Hegel, G.W.F. 1977. *The Phenomenology of Spirit*. Translated by A.V. Miller. Oxford: Clarendon Press.

Hill, Thomas, Jr. 2000. *Respect, Pluralism and Justice: Kantian Perspectives*. Oxford and New York: Oxford University Press.

Hyde, Lewis. 1983. *The Gift: Imagination and the Erotic Life of Property*. New York: Vintage.

Irigaray, Luce. 1996. *I Love to You: Sketch of A Possible Felicity in History*. Translated by Alison Martin. New York: Routledge Press.

Johnson, Mark. 1993. *Moral Imagination: Implications of Cognitive Science for Ethics*. Chicago: University of Chicago Press.

―――. 1989. *The Body in the Mind: The Bodily Basis of Meaning, Imagination and Reason*. Chicago: University of Chicago Press.

Kant, Immanuel. 1987. *Critique of Judgment*. Translated by Werner S. Pluhar. Indianapolis: Hackett.

Kateb, George. Editor. 1971. *Utopia*. New York: Atherton Press.

Kearney, Richard. 1988. *The Wake of Imagination*. Minneapolis: University of Minnesota Press.

————. 1984. *Dialogues With Contemporary Continental Thinkers: Stanislov Breton, Jacques Derrida, Emmanuel Levinas, Herbert Marcuse, and Paul Ricoeur*. Manchester: Manchester University Press.

Kierkegaard, Søren. 1985. *Philosophical Fragments and Johannes Climacus*. Translated by Howard Hong and Edna Hong. Princeton: Princeton University Press.

————. 1983. *Fear and Trembling/Repetition: Kierkegaard's Writings*, Vol. 6. Translated by Howard Hong and Edna Hong. Princeton: Princeton University Press.

King, Martin Luther Jr. 1991a. "Love, Law, and Civil Disobedience." In *A Testament of Hope: The Essential Writings and Speeches of Martin Luther King Jr*. Edited by James Washington. San Francisco: HarperCollins.

————. 1991b. "An Address Before the National Press Club." In *A Testament of Hope: The Essential Writings and Speeches of Martin Luther King, Jr*. Edited by James Washington. San Francisco: HarperCollins.

————. 1991c. "Facing the Challenge of the New Age." In *A Testament of Hope: The Essential Writings and Speeches of Martin Luther King, Jr*. Edited by James Washington. San Francisco: HarperCollins.

Kumar, Krishnan. 1991. *Utopianism*. Minneapolis: University of Minnesota Press.

Lakoff, Georg. 1990. *Women, Fire, and Dangerous Things*. Chicago: University of Chicago Press.

Lakoff, George and Mark Johnson. 1980. *Metaphors We Live By*. Chicago: University of Chicago Press.

Levin, David Michael. 1990. "Justice in the Flesh." In *Ontology and Alterity in Merleau-Ponty*. Edited by Galen A. Johnson and Michael B. Smith. Evanston: Northwestern University Press.

————. 1988. *The Opening of Vision: Nihilism and the Postmodern Situation.* London: Routledge, Kegan & Paul.

————. 1985. *The Body's Recollection of Being.* London: Routledge, Kegan & Paul.

Levinas, Emmanuel. 1981. *Otherwise than Being or Beyond Essence.* Translated by Alphonso Lingis. Boston: Martinus Nijhoff.

Levitas, Ruth. 1990. *The Concept of Utopia.* New York: Syracuse University Press.

Lyotard, Jean-François. 1984. *The Postmodern Condition: A Report on Knowledge.* Translated by G. Bennington and B. Massumi. Minneapolis: University of Minnesota Press.

Madison, Gary. 1990. "Flesh as Otherness." In *Ontology and Alterity in Merleau-Ponty.* Edited by Galen A. Johnson and Michael B. Smith. Evanston: Northwestern University Press.

————. 1988. *The Hermeneutics of Postmodernity: Figures and Themes.* Indianapolis: Indiana University Press.

Manuel, Frank and Fritzie. 1979. *Utopian Thought in the Western World.* Cambridge: Belknap/Harvard Press.

Marcel, Gabriel. 1964. *Creative Fidelity.* Translated by Robert Rosthal. New York: Farrar, Strauss and Company.

Marty, Martin. 1992. *"Grace." A New Handbook of Christian Theology.* Edited by D.W. Musser & J.L. Price. Nashville: Abingdon Press.

Merleau-Ponty, Maurice. 1969. *Humanism and Terror.* Boston: Beacon Press.

————. 1968. *The Visible and the Invisible.* Edited by Claude Lefort. Translated by Alphonso Lingis. Evanston: Northwestern University Press.

————. 1964a. *Sense and Non-Sense.* Translated by H.L. and P.A. Dreyfus. Evanston: Northwestern University Press.

————. 1964b. *Signs.* Translated by R.C. McCleary. Evanston: Northwestern University Press.

————. 1962. *Phenomenology of Perception.* Translated by Colin Smith. New York: Routledge.

Miles, Angela. 1996. *Integrative Feminisms: Building Global Visions,* 1960s-1990s. New York and London: Routledge.

Moi, Toril . 1993. "Beauvoir's Utopia: The Politics of The Second Sex." *The South Atlantic Quarterly.* 92, No 2 (Spring): 210-242.

Montaigne, Michel De. 1987. *The Complete Essays.* Translated by M.A. Screech. New York: Penguin Press.

Oakeshott, Michael. 1977. *Rationalism and Politics.* London: Methuen.

Plaskow, Judith. 1980. *Sex, Sin and Grace: The Concepts in Reinhold Niebuhr and Paul Tillich.* Chicago: University Press of America.

Plato. 1993. *The Symposium and The Phaedrus: Plato's Erotic Dialogues.* Translated by William S. Cobb. Albany : State University of New York Press.

Pogge, Thomas. 2001. "How Should Human Rights Be Conceived?" In *The Philosophy of Human Rights.* Edited by Patrick Hayden. St. Paul: Paragon House.

Polanyi, Michael. 1962. *Personal Knowledge.* Chicago: University of Chicago Press.

Rawls, John. 1993. *Political Liberalism.* New York: Columbia University Press.

———. 1974. *A Theory of Justice.* Cambridge, MA.: Harvard University Press.

Reagon, Bernice Johnson. 1983. "Coalition Politics: Turning the Century." In *Home Girls: A Black Feminist Anthology.* Edited by Barbara Smith. New York: Kitchen Table: Women of Color Press.

Ricoeur, Paul. 1986. *Lectures on Ideology and Utopia.* Edited by George H. Taylor. New York: Columbia University Press.

———. 1980. "The Hermeneutics of Testimony." In *Essays on Biblical Interpretation.* Edited by Lewis Mudge. Philadelphia: Fortress Press.

———. 1976. *Interpretation Theory: Discourse and the Surplus of Meaning.* Fort Worth: Texas Christian University Press.

Shriver, Donald. 1998. "Is There Forgiveness in Politics?" In *Exploring Forgiveness.* Edited by Robert D. Enright and Joanna North. Madison: University of Wisconsin Press.

Scott, Charles. 1997. *On the Advantages and Disadvantages of Ethics and Politics*. Bloomington and Indianapolis: Indiana University Press.

Slaughter, Thomas. 1984. "Epidermalizing the World: A Basic Mode of Being Black." In *Philosophy Born of Struggle*. Edited by Leonard Harris. Dubuque: Hunt Press.

Sölle, Dorothee. 1990. *Thinking about God*. London: SCM Press.

Taylor, Mark. C. 2007. *After God*. Chicago, IL.: University of Chicago Press.

Tutu, Desmond. 1998. "Without Forgiveness There is No Future." In *Exploring Forgiveness*. Edited by Robert D. Enright and Joanna North. Madison: University of Wisconsin Press.

Vattimo. Gianni. 2006. "Utopia Dispersed." *Diogenes*. 53, No. 1, 18-23.

———. 2004. *Nihilism and Emancipation*. Translated by William McCuaig. New York: Columbia University Press.

———. 2002. *After Christianity*. Translated by Luca D'Isanto. New York: Columbia University Press.

West, Cornel. 1994. *Race Matters*. New York: Vintage Books.

———. 1993. *Keeping Faith: Philosophy and Race in America*. New York: Routledge.

Williams, Bernard. 2005. *In the Beginning was the Deed: Realism and Moralism in Political Argument*. New Jersey: Princeton University Press.

———. 2002. *Truth and Truthfulness: An Essay in Genealogy*. New Jersey: Princeton University Press.

Young, Iris Marion. 1997a. *Intersecting Voices: Dilemmas of Gender, Political Philosophy, and Policy*. Princeton, NJ: Princeton University Press.

———. 1997b "Asymmetrical Reciprocity: On Moral Respect, Wonder, and Enlarged Thought." *Constellations: An International Journal of Critical and Democratic Theory*. 3, No. 3 (October): 87-111.

———. 1996. "Communication and the Other: Beyond Deliberative Democracy." In *Democracy and Difference: Contesting the Boundaries of the Political*. Edited by Seyla Benhabib. New Jersey: Princeton University Press.

————. 1994. "Comments on Seyla Benhabib, Situating the Self." *New German Critique*. 62 (Spring-Summer): 126-140.

————. 1990a. *Justice and the Politics of Difference*. Princeton, New Jersey: Princeton University Press.

————. 1990b. *Throwing Like a Girl and Other Essays in Feminist Philosophy and Social Theory*. Indianapolis: Indiana University Press.

Žižek, Slavoj. 2008. "The Ambiguity of the Utopian Gaze." *Umbr(a): A Journal of the Unconscious*. New York: State University of New York/ Buffalo.

————. Editor. 2002. *Revolution at the Gates: Žižek on Lenin, the 1917 Writings*. London and New York: Verso Press.

Index

Ackerman, Bruce, 173–174
Arendt, Hannah, 81–85, 87–
  88,93–95, 100, 102–103, 130,
  149–153, 173

Benhabib, Seyla, x–xi, 83, 85–95,
  102–104, 119–121, 169,
  173–174
Bernasconi, Robert, 170–171
Bernstein, Richard J., 85, 119, 173
Biehl, Amy, 21, 146–148, 150, 166
Biehl, John and Mary, 146–148,
  150, 165–167
Boff, Leonardo, 35

Caputo, John, 152–153, 170, 172
Cash, Johnny, 141–142
Cavell, Stanley, 162–164
Coalition politics, 105, 108
Code, Lorraine, 172
Cognitive Linguistics, 29–30, 170
Colapietro, Vincent, 113
Coles, Romand, 174
Collins, Patricia Hill, 78
Conceptual metaphor, 16, 29–30,
  38–39, 40–41, 47
Consistency (in action), 20, 124,
  139–141
Cornell, Drucilla, 1, 3–4, 25, 169
Critchley, Simon, x–xi, xv, 17, 20,
  51–54, 124, 126–127, 138,
  170–171
Critical Social Theory, x, xiv, 4–5,
  10, 23, 51–52, 169, 171
Critique, 1, 3, 6, 11, 23, 27, 60, 87,
  90, 128, 130, 169, 173

D'Souza, Corinne Kumar, 121

Dahrendorf, Ralf, 11–12
Das Leben der Anderen (The Lives
  of Others), 132
Deliberative Democracy, 19, 21,
  125, 145, 154–156, 159, 167
Derrida, Jacques, 26–27, 53–55, 91,
  150–151, 170–172
Desmond, William, 170
Dewey, John, 151, 174
Dillon, M.C., 172
Donskis, Leonidis, 12
Du Toit, André, 160

Enlarged thinking, 83–85, 87–91,
  94, 187
Existentialism, 141–142
Ethical, xi–xii, 2, 4, 12, 16, 25, 40,
  49, 81–83, 102–104, 106, 109,
  115, 126–127, 131, 138–139, 149,
  151–152, 156, 164–166, 172
Ethics, 5, 57, 83, 85, 89, 94, 101,
  124, 127–128, 134, 136,
  171–172
Eros, 27
Erotic, 27–28, 116–117

Feminism, 1, 5, 7, 19, 117, 121–123,
  140
Feminist, 5–7, 14, 38, 104, 169, 175
Fidelity, 20, 23, 68, 124–127, 138,
  141–142
Frye, Northrop, 17, 55
Forgiveness, 21, 27, 32–33, 36, 49,
  145ff

Gibbs, Raymond, 29
Gill, Jerry, 61, 174
Goodwin, Barbara, 5, 8, 10, 13

Grace, 16, 29–41, 44, 47–49, 124,
     153, 165, 167, 170
Guignon, Charles, 142
Gutmann, Amy, 155–161, 164–
     166, 175

Habel, Norman, 45
Harris, Leonard, 173
Hegel, G.W.F., xii, 137, 174–175
Heidegger, Martin, 5, 128, 131,
     135, 169
Hermeneutics, x–xi, xiv, 4, 17, 19,
     24, 51–52, 108, 128, 130–131,
     134, 171
Hill, Thomas, Jr., 171
Hyde, Lewis, 116–117

Ideology, x, 10
Imagination, 9, 26, 73
Integrative feminism, 19, 117,
     121–122, 140
Interpretation, 19, 41, 62, 84,
     100, 108, 116–119, 123, 125,
     127–130, 133–135, 137, 139,
     142, 155, 158, 171, 173
Irigaray, Luce, 53–55, 171

Job, 45–49
Johnson, Mark, 29, 42, 120, 170,
     172
Justice, 21, 43–44, 46, 80, 82, 89,
     92, 126, 145, 148, 150, 153–
     155, 158–161, 165–167, 170

Kant, Immanuel, 54, 83, 88, 123,
     130, 136, 171, 173
Kateb, George, 1–4
Kearney, Richard, 10, 23
Kierkegaard, Søren, 57, 128, 131,
     175

King, Martin Luther Jr., 2–4, 115
Kumar, Krishnan, 9, 15, 169

Lakoff, George, 29
Levin, David Michael, 57, 60, 77,
     97–98, 100, 172
Levinas, Emmanuel, 57, 172
Levitas, Ruth, 8, 169
Lyotard, Jean–François, xi, 16

Madison, Gary, 98, 171–172
Manuel, Frank and Fritz, 169
Marcel, Gabriel, 125–126
Marty, Martin, 35–36
Merleau-Ponty, Maurice, x, xiv–
     xv, 18, 26, 52, 55–77, 80–83,
     95–97, 99–102, 104–110, 169,
     171–172, 174
Metaphor, 16, 29–31, 36, 40–49,
     141, 153, 165, 170
Miles, Angela, 122–123
Moi, Toril, 5–7, 169
Morality, 16, 42, 88, 120

Nietzsche, Friedrich, 128–131
Nihilism, 128, 134–135, 137–138

Oakeshott, Michael, 11

Pathos, 26–28, 79
Pereboom, Derk, 142
Phenomenology, x–xi, xiv, xvii,
     4, 17, 20, 24, 51–52, 54–55,
     60–61, 66–67, 96, 98, 169–
     172, 175
Plaskow, Judith, 38
Plato, 9, 23, 27–28, 170
Pogge, Thomas, 9
Polanyi, Michael, 172, 174
Political, x–xii, xiv, 2–8, 12, 14, 16,

17, 19–20, 23, 25, 40, 49, 54,
56, 79, 81, 83, 85, 87, 89–90,
94, 97–98, 101, 105–106, 108–
109, 115, 118–120, 122, 126,
128, 131, 138–139, 141–143,
145–146, 149, 151–161, 164,
173–174

Rawls, John, 9, 89, 156, 173
Reagon, Bernice Johnson, 105–
108, 174
Reciprocity, 18–19, 60, 85–87, 90,
93–94, 96, 101–104, 117, 120,
152, 155–167, 174–175
Religion, 23, 120, 129
Responsibility, 31, 39–40, 79, 86,
123–124, 128, 137, 140–142,
152, 154, 172
Ricoeur, Paul, x–xi, xiv, 19, 23, 100,
113–114, 117, 140, 171, 175
Rousseau, Jean–Jacques, 9, 11, 15,
175

Sartre, Jean–Paul, 141–142, 172
Shriver, Donald, 154, 175
Scott, Charles, 63, 95, 101
Slaughter, Thomas, 173
Sölle, Dorothee, 38
South African Truth and
Reconciliation Commission,
20, 49, 110, 125, 145, 155, 160

Taylor, Mark. C., 126
Testimony, 19–20, 35, 89, 108, 111,
113–118, 123, 125, 130, 139,
142–143, 148, 153–154, 165
Thompson, Dennis, 155–161,
164–166, 175
Truth, Sojourner, 17, 58, 78–79, 89,
118, 140, 147

Truthfulness, 19–20, 111, 114,
124, 138,141
Tutu, Desmond, 149–150, 152, 154

Universal, x–xii, 2, 10, 12, 15–16,
18–20, 25, 35, 38, 41, 47, 59,
61–62, 64, 68, 79–82, 85, 88–
90, 96–99, 101, 104, 107–111,
115–125, 127, 130, 136, 138,
140, 167, 175
Utopian (conventional), xiii,, 6–9,
12, 15–18, 23–24, 26, 53–56,
63, 82–83, 118–119, 128, 131,
171–172

Vattimo. Gianni, xv, 20, 126–135,
137–138

Weak Thought, 128–129
West, Cornel, 3, 83, 162–163
WHISPER (Women Hurt
in Systems of Prostitution
Engaged in Revolt), 122–123,
147
Williams, Bernard, 138–139, 175
Wittgenstein, 137
Young, Iris Marion, 65–66, 75–77,
83, 90–95, 97,103–104, 169,
173–174

Žižek, Slavoj, 28–29, 170

Made in the USA
Lexington, KY
06 March 2011